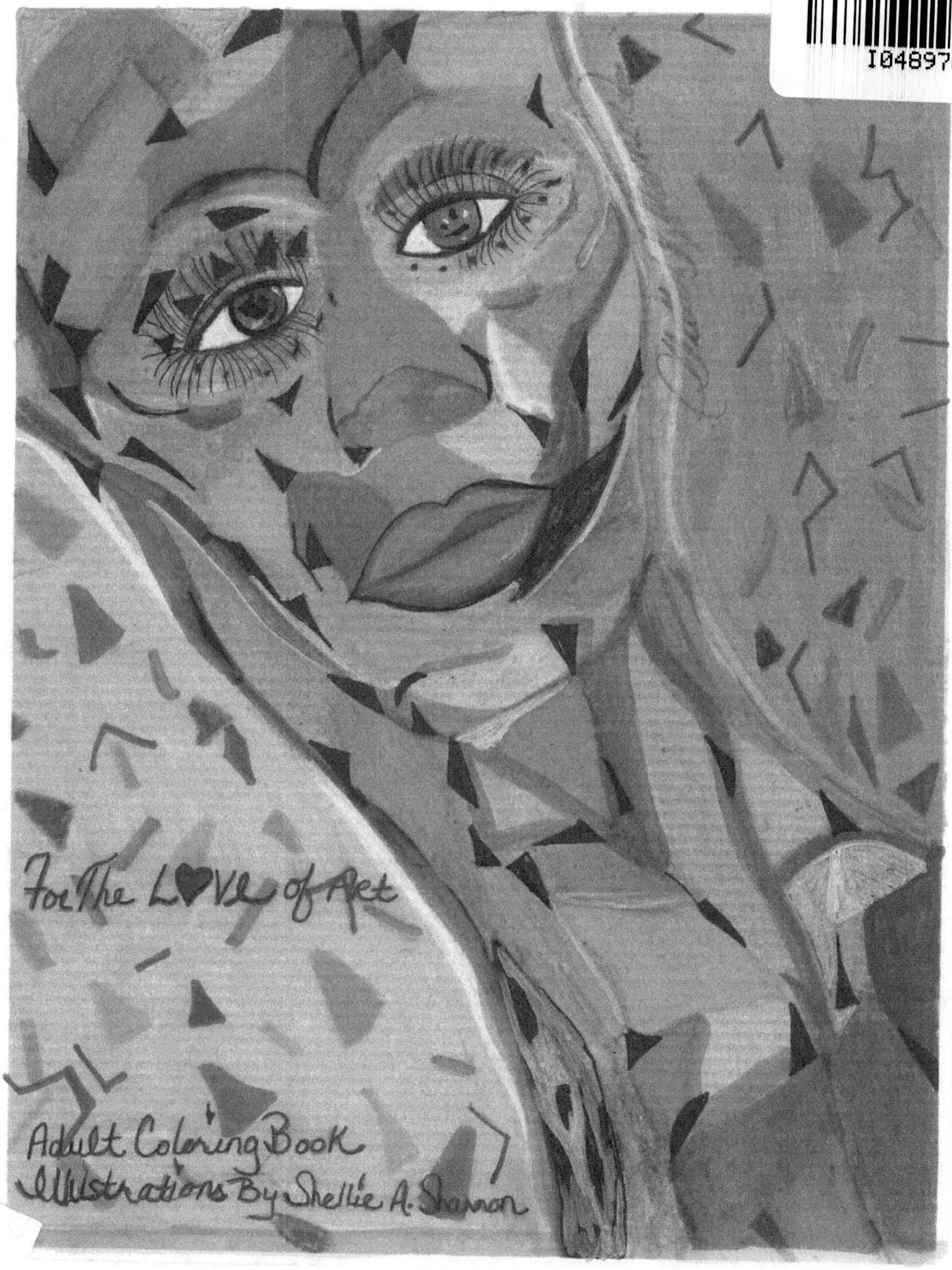
For The LOVE of Art
Adult Coloring Book
Illustrations By Shellie A. Shannon

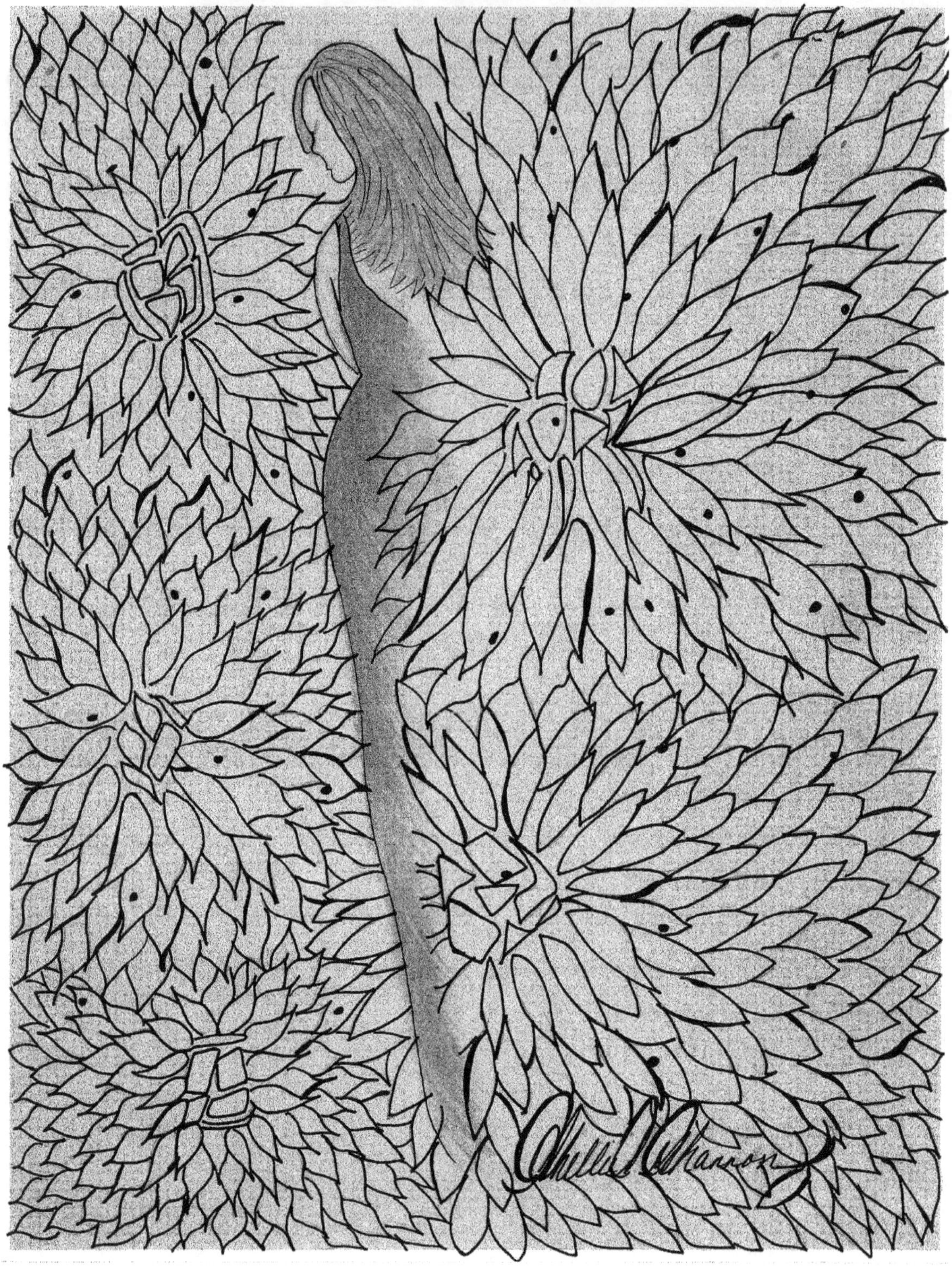

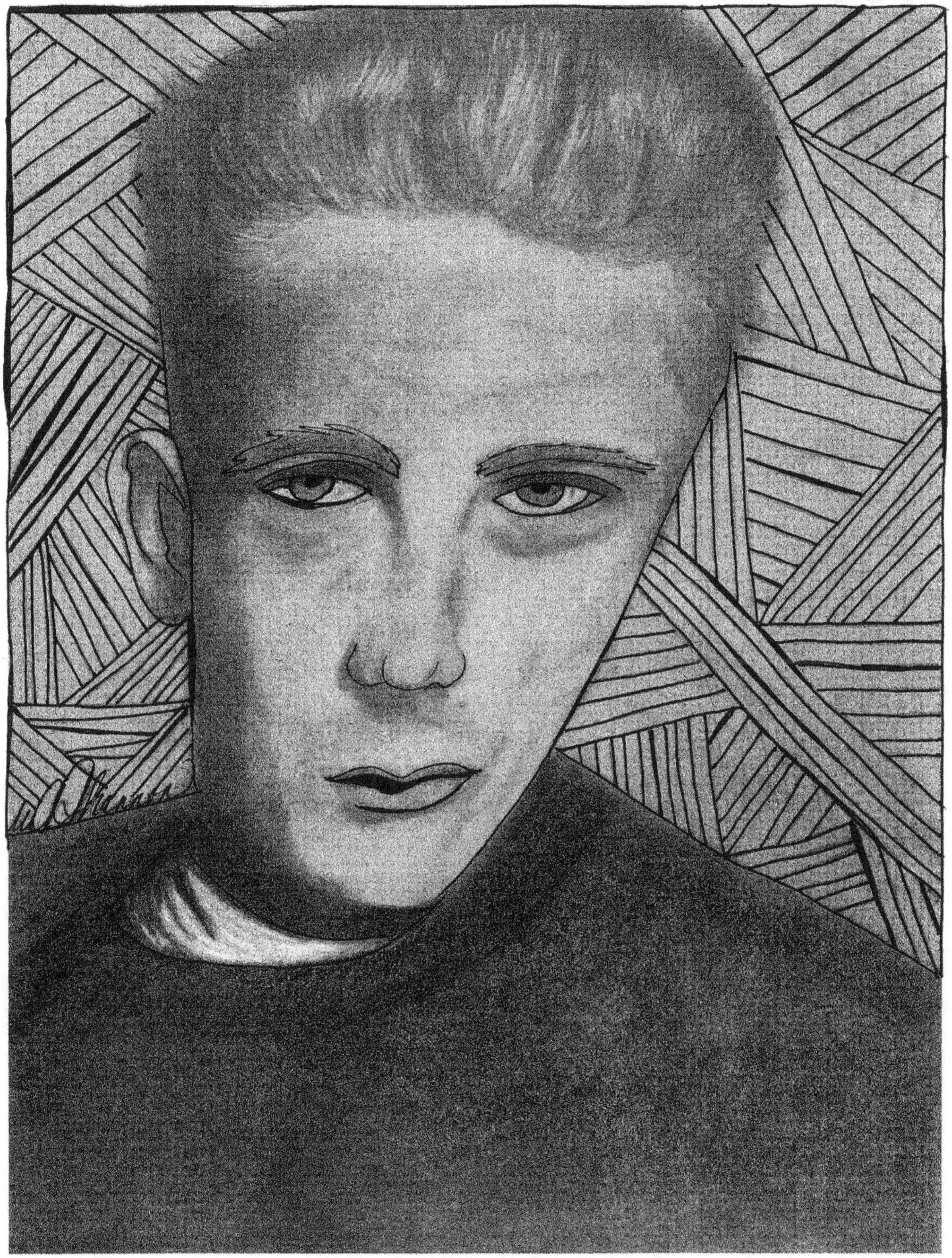

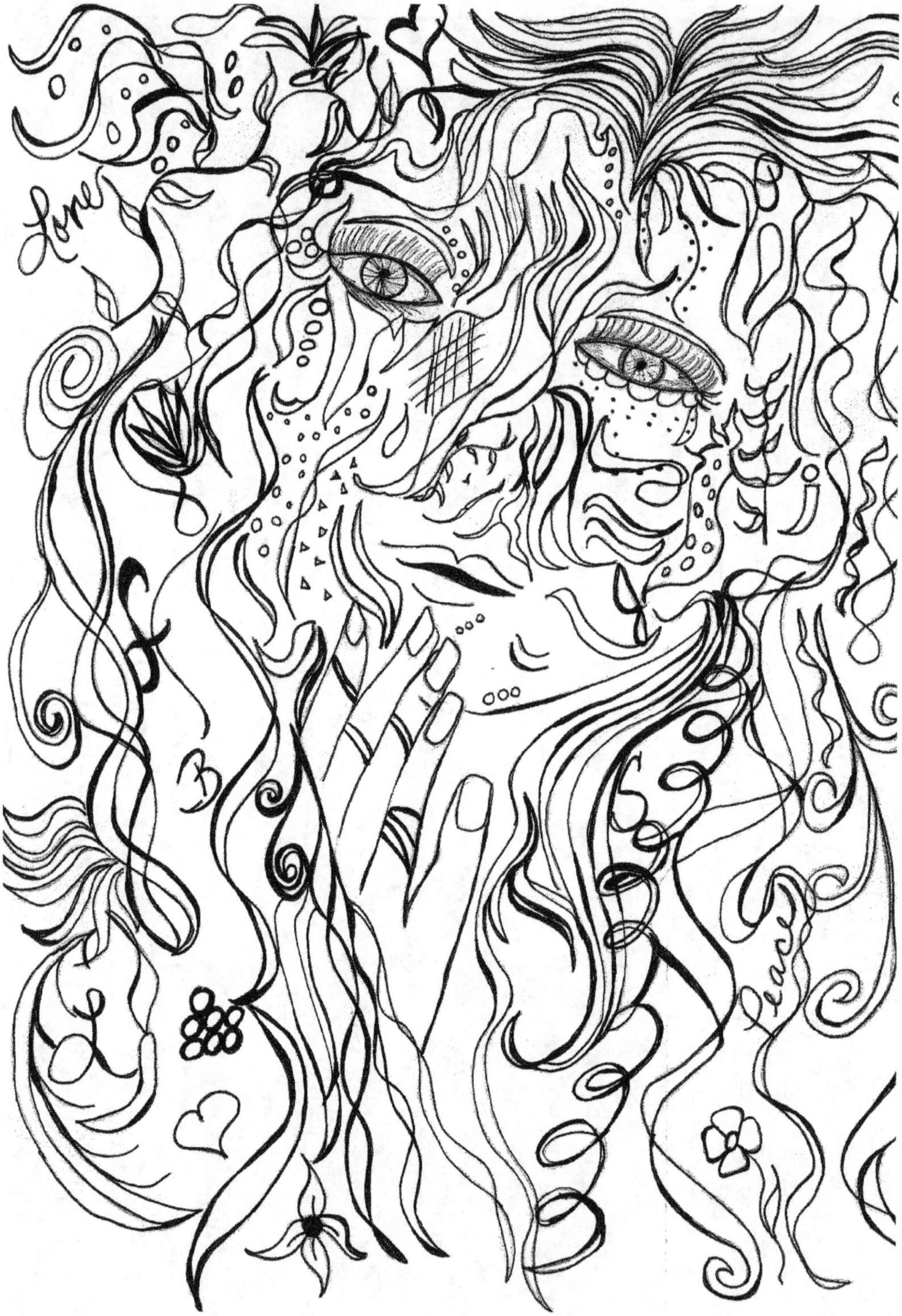
Love
Peace

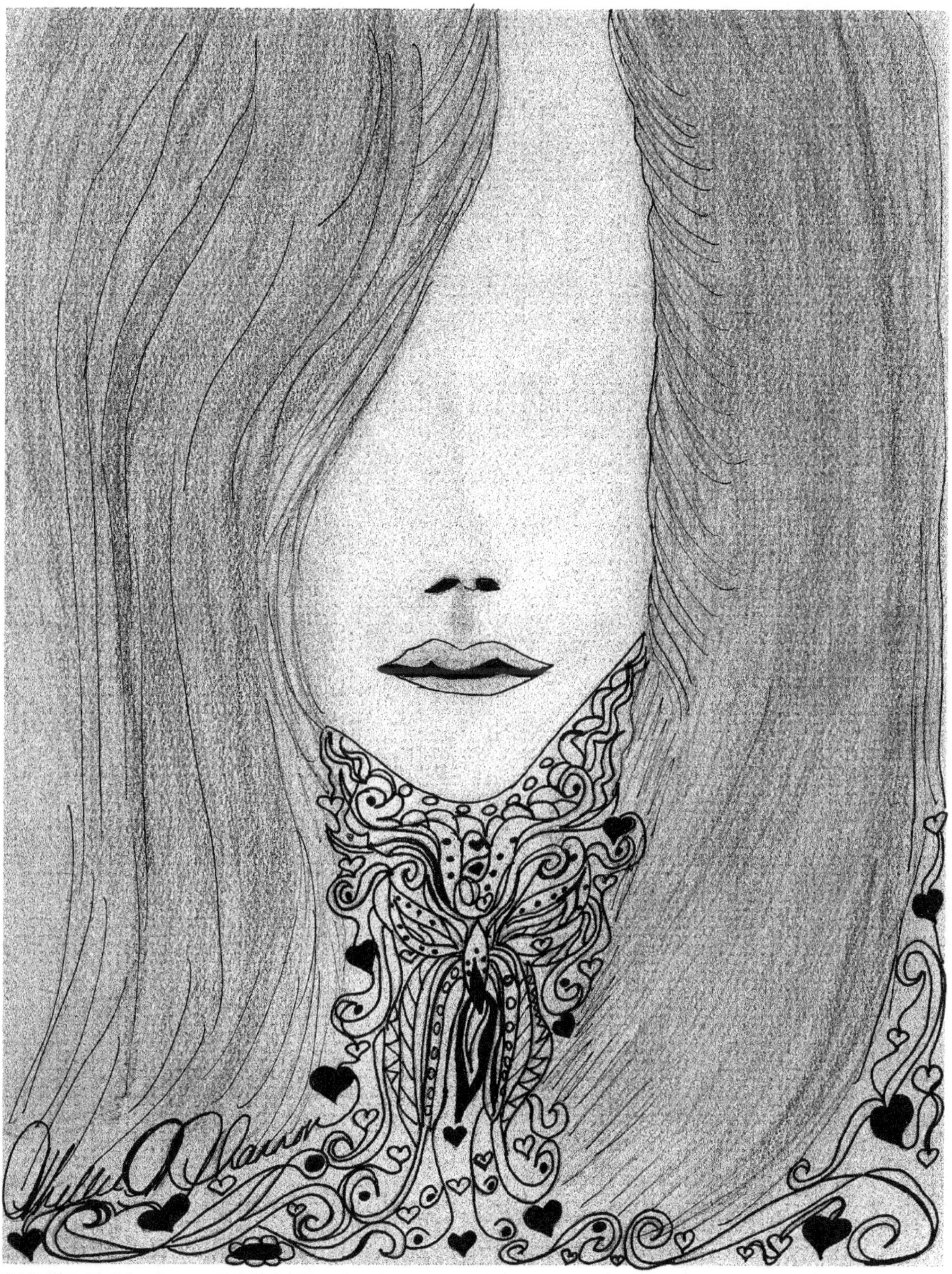

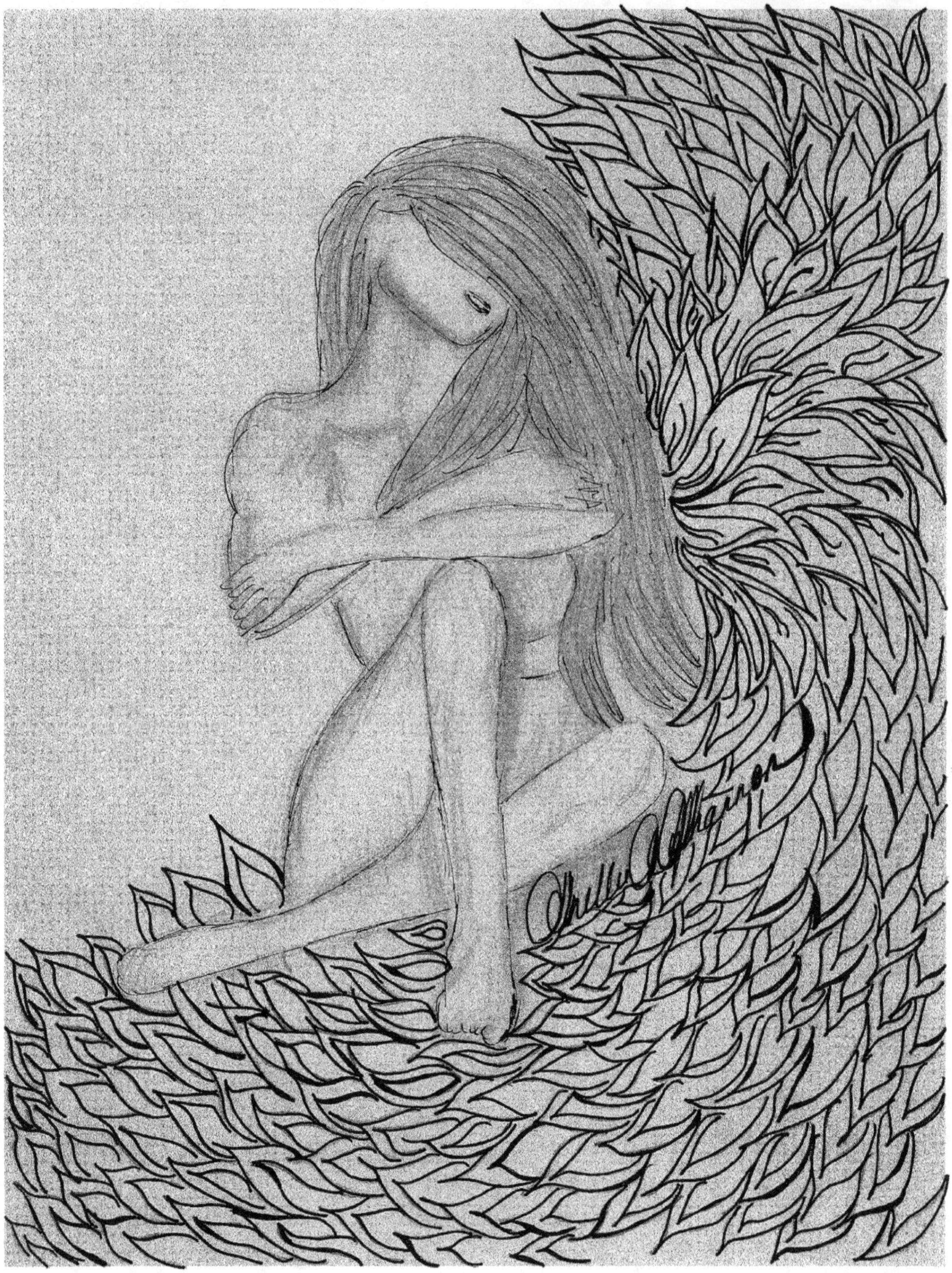

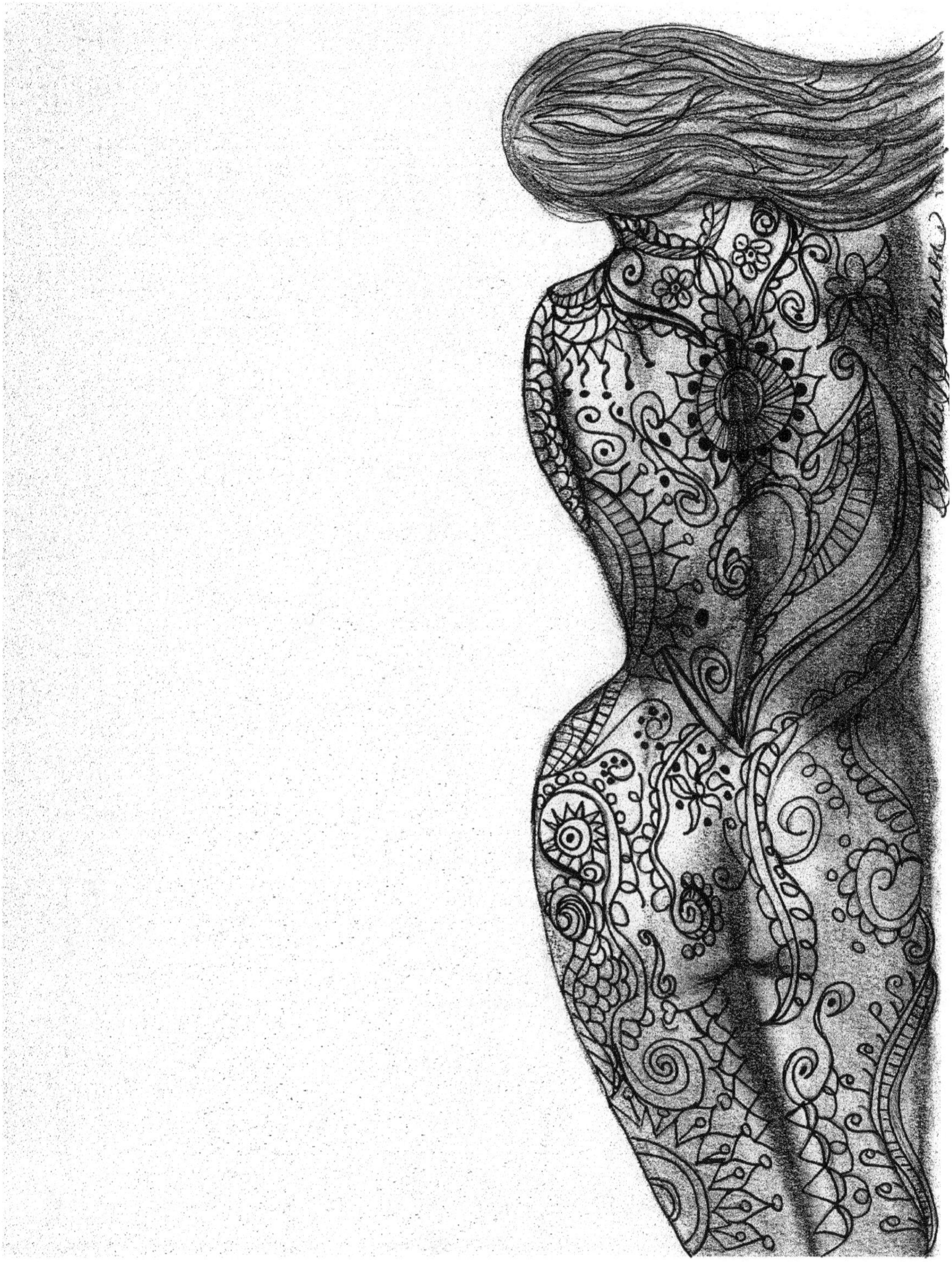

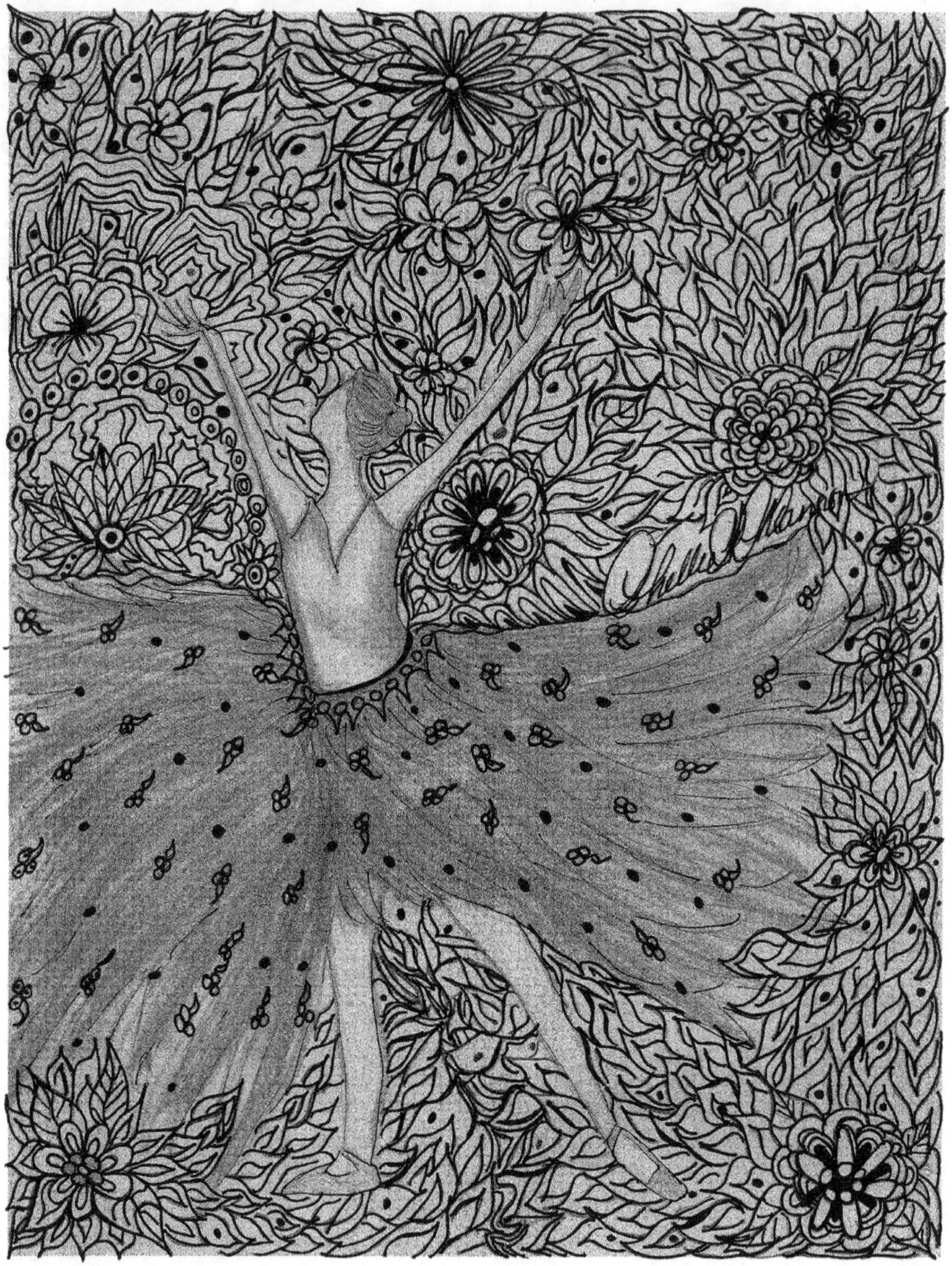

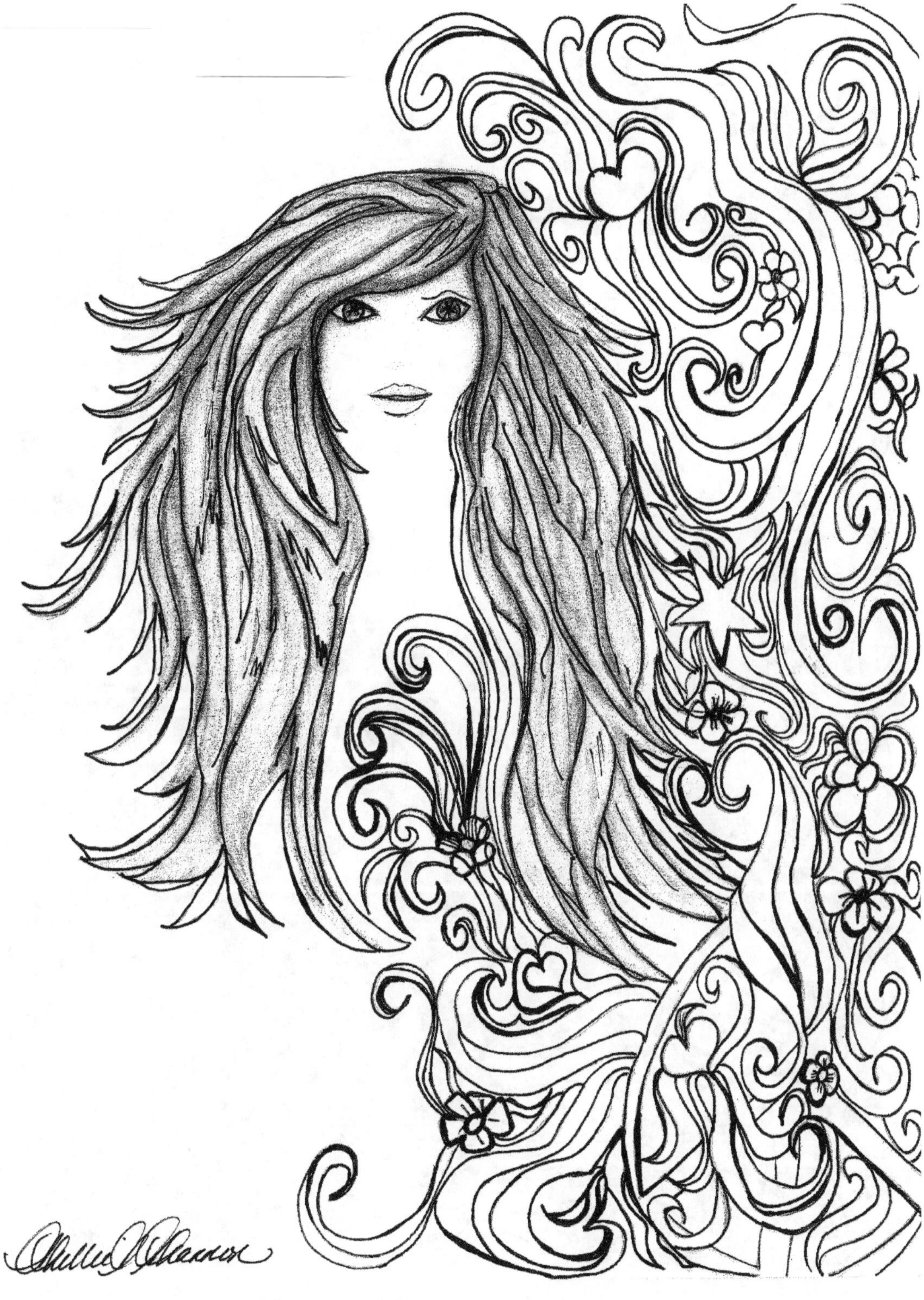

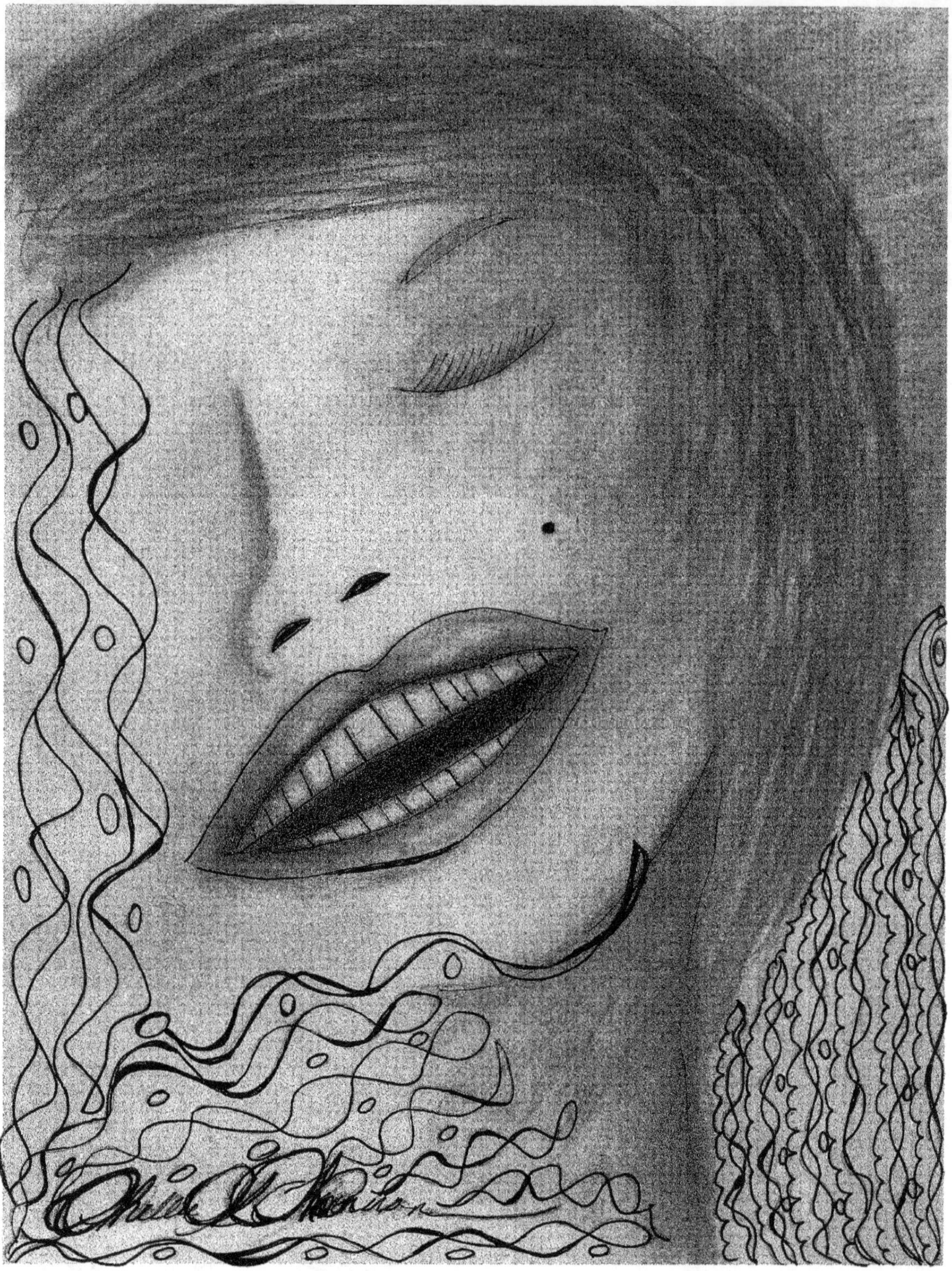

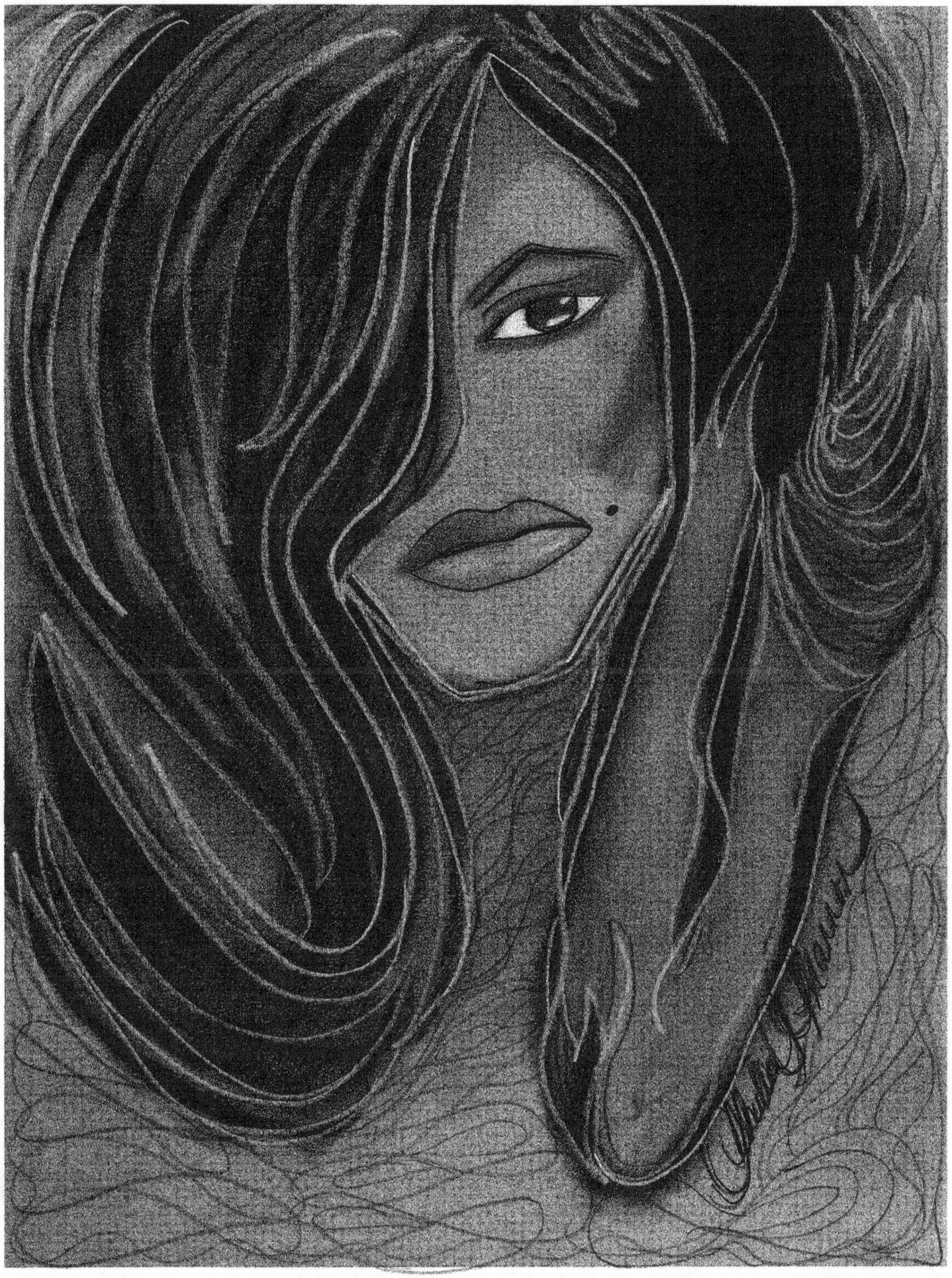

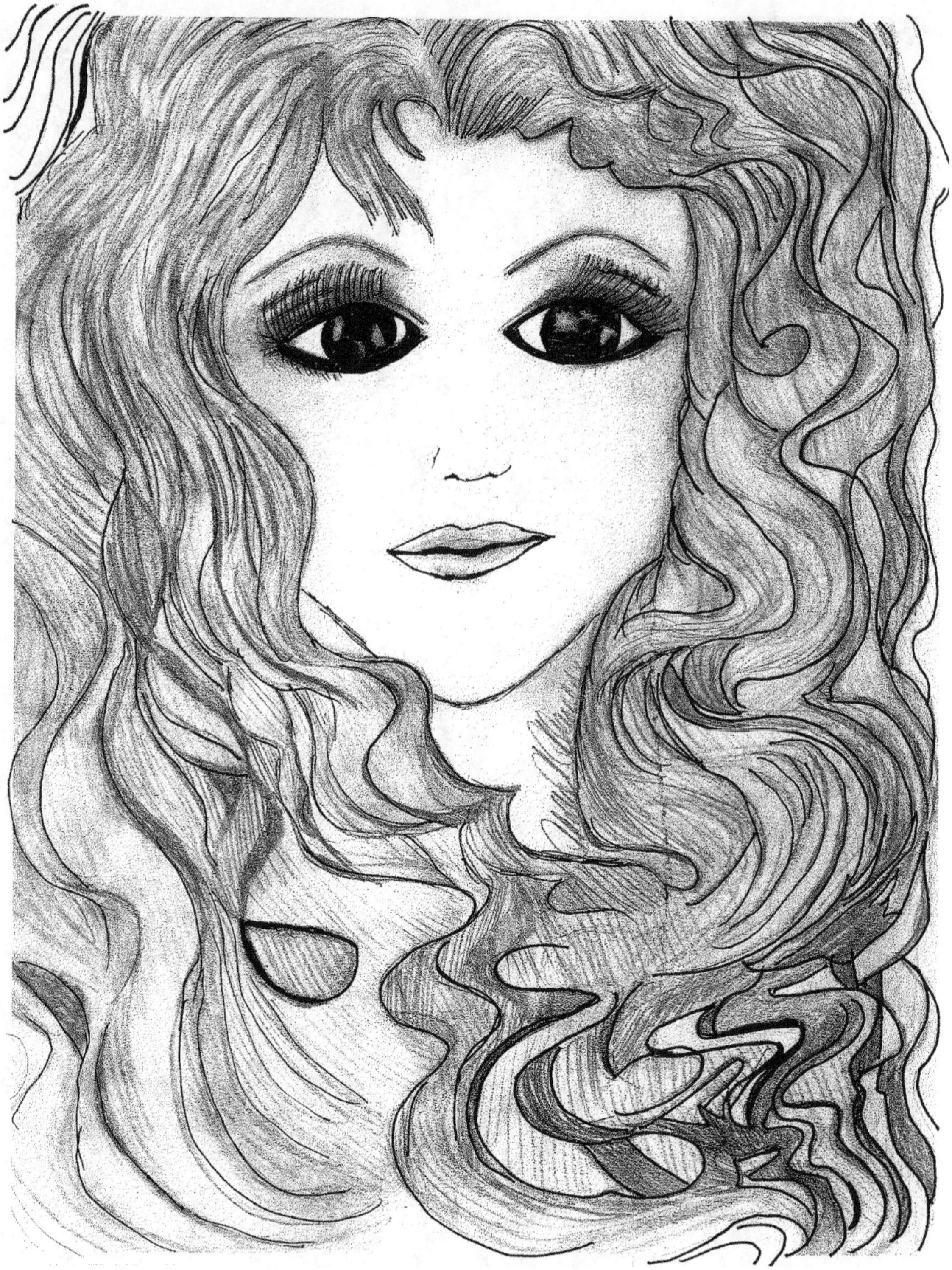

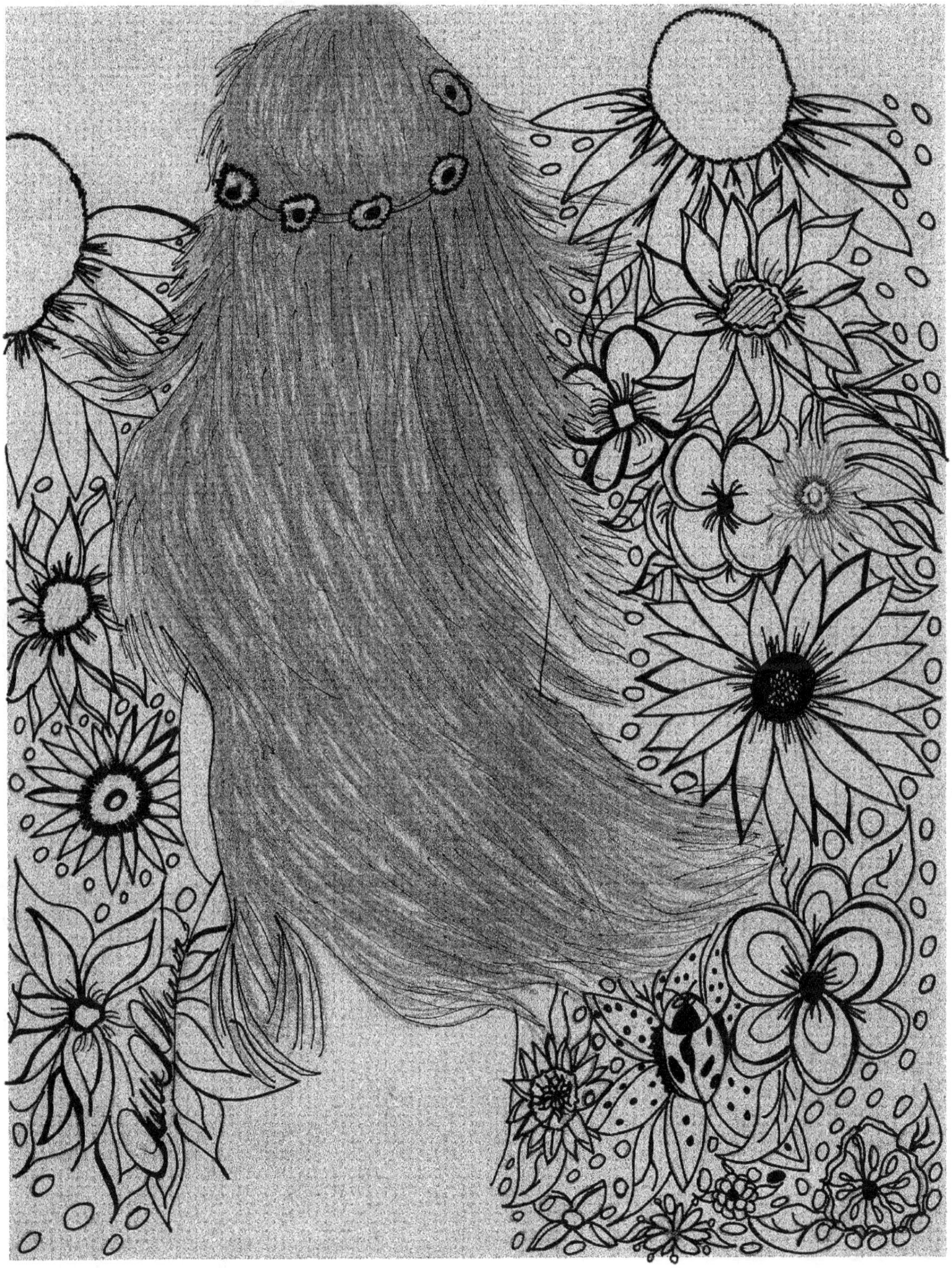

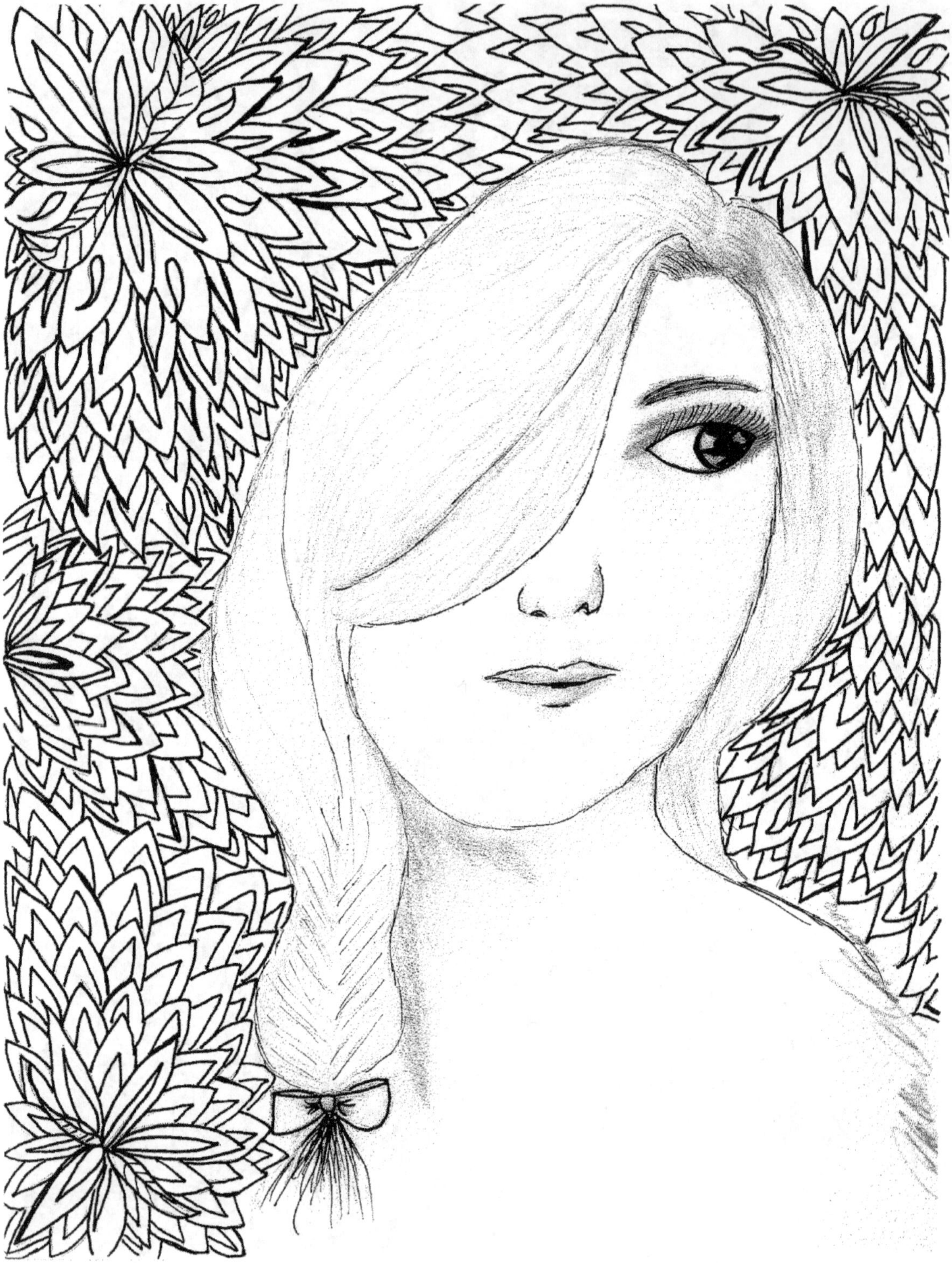

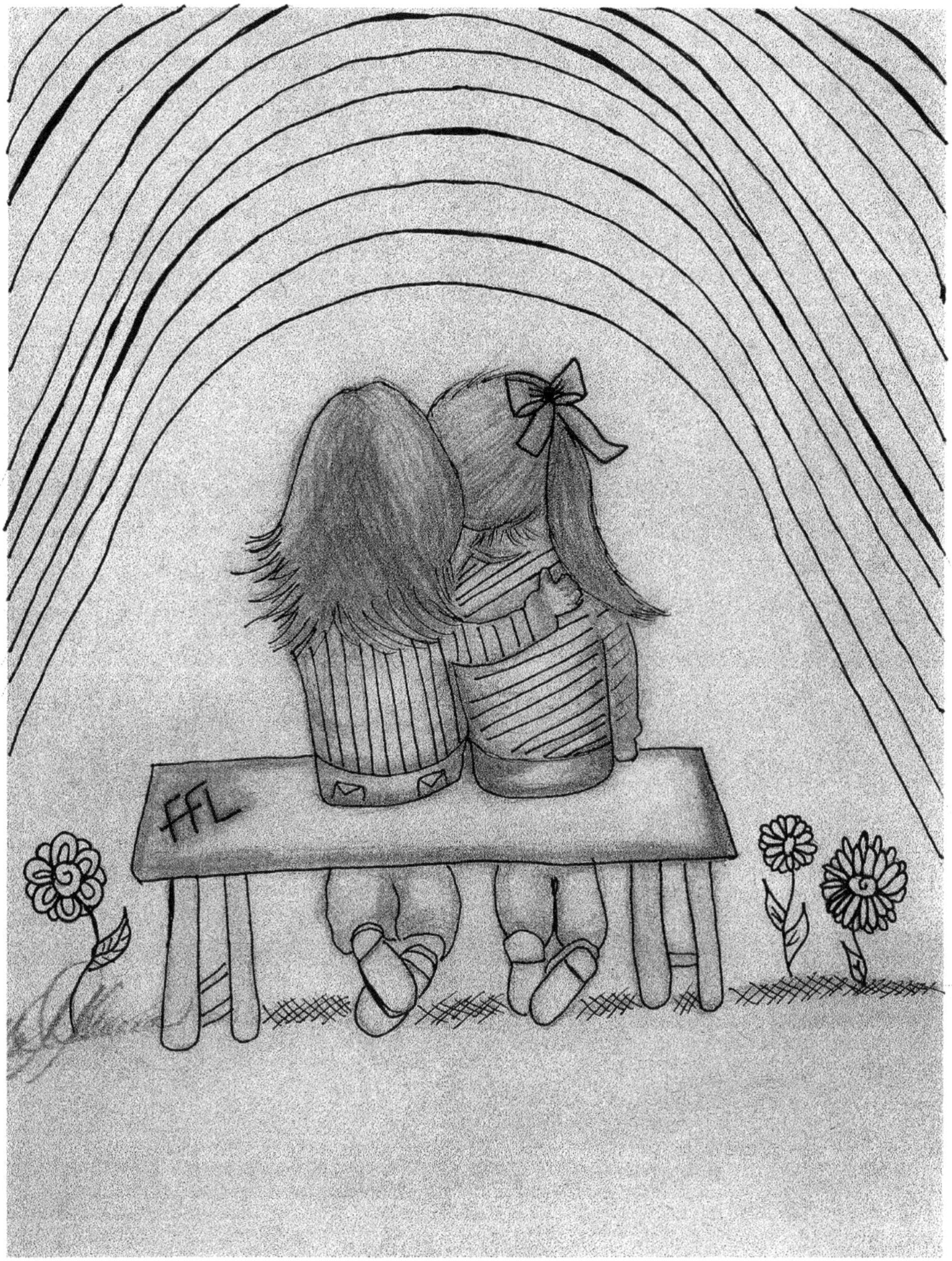
FFL

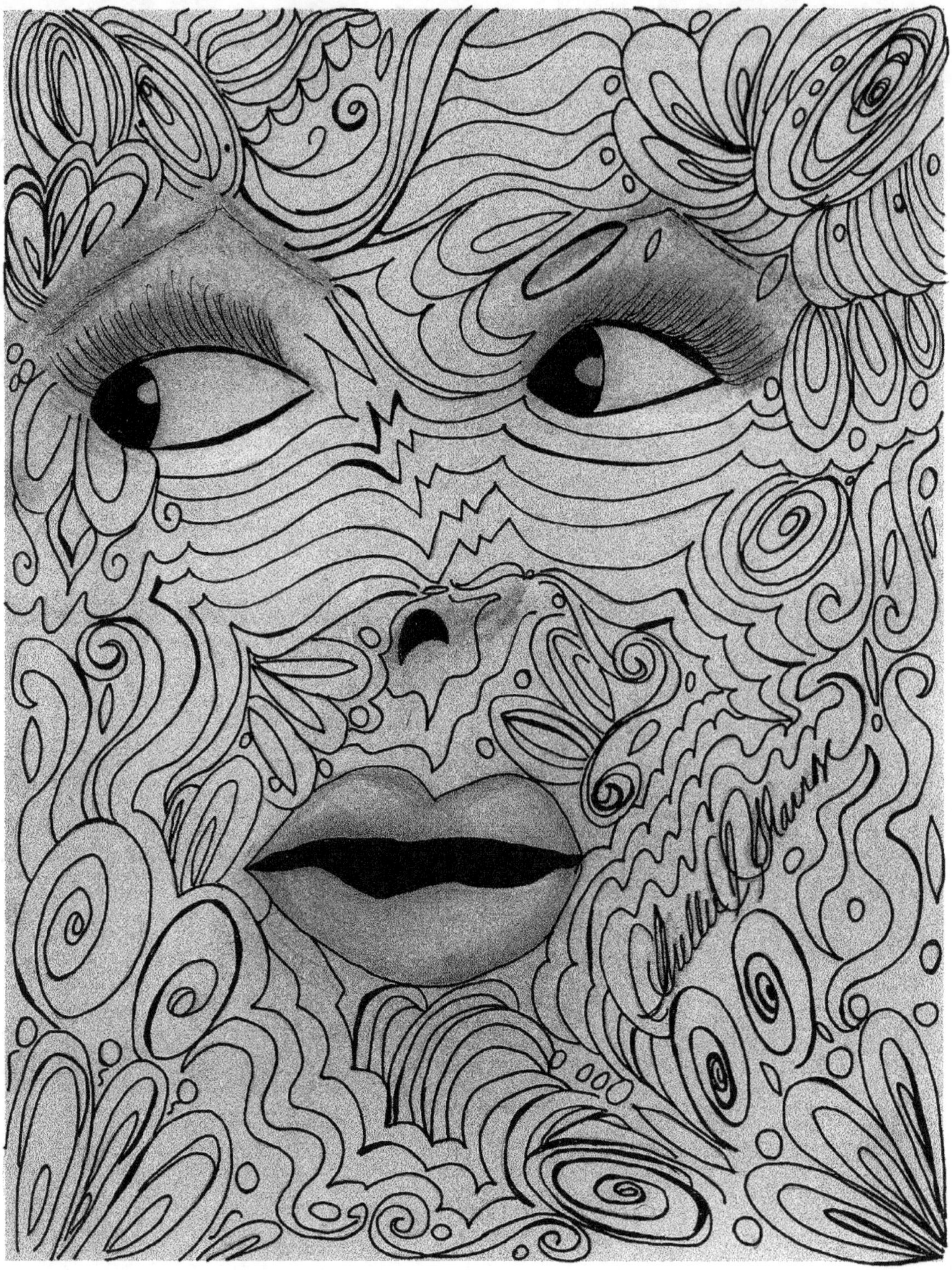

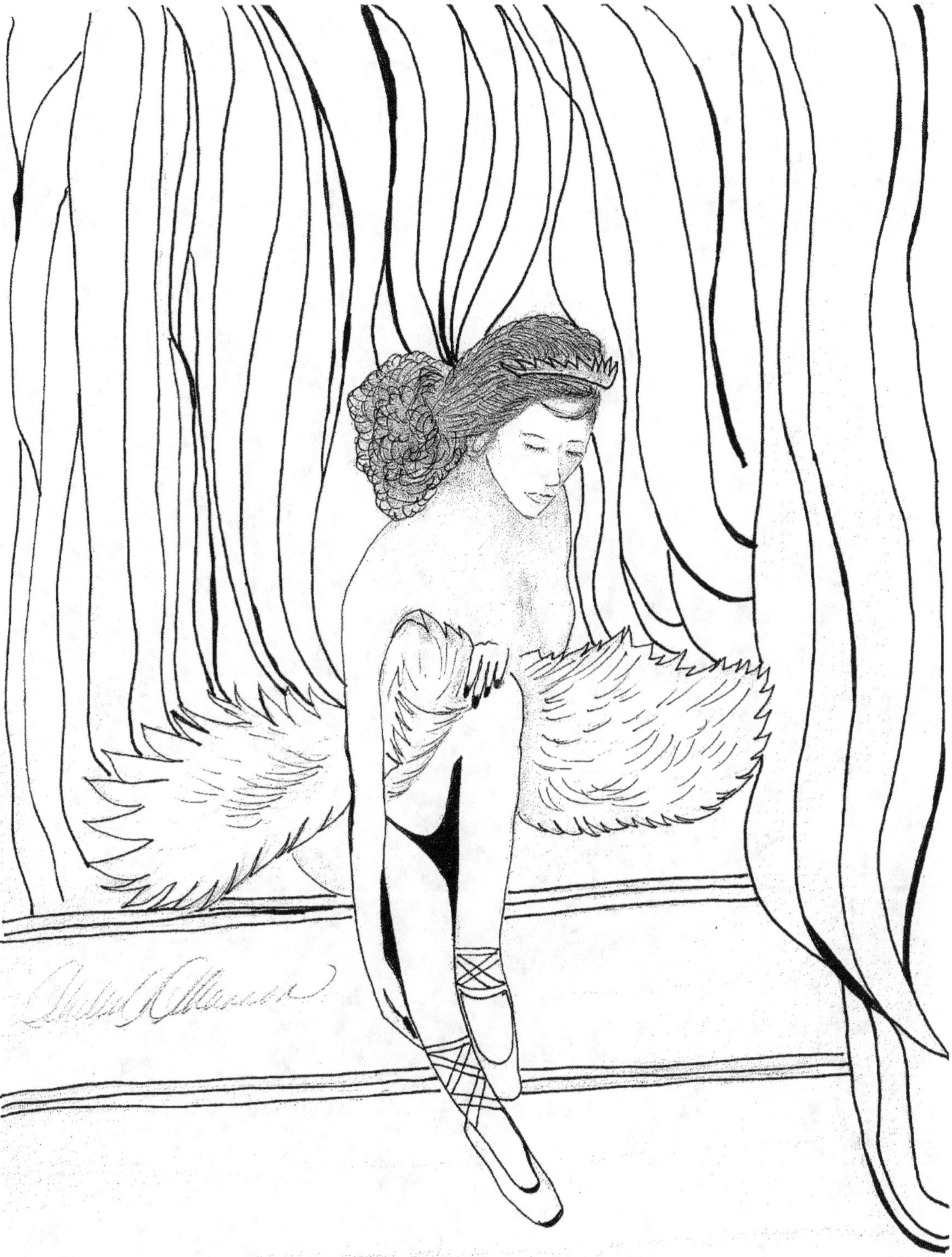

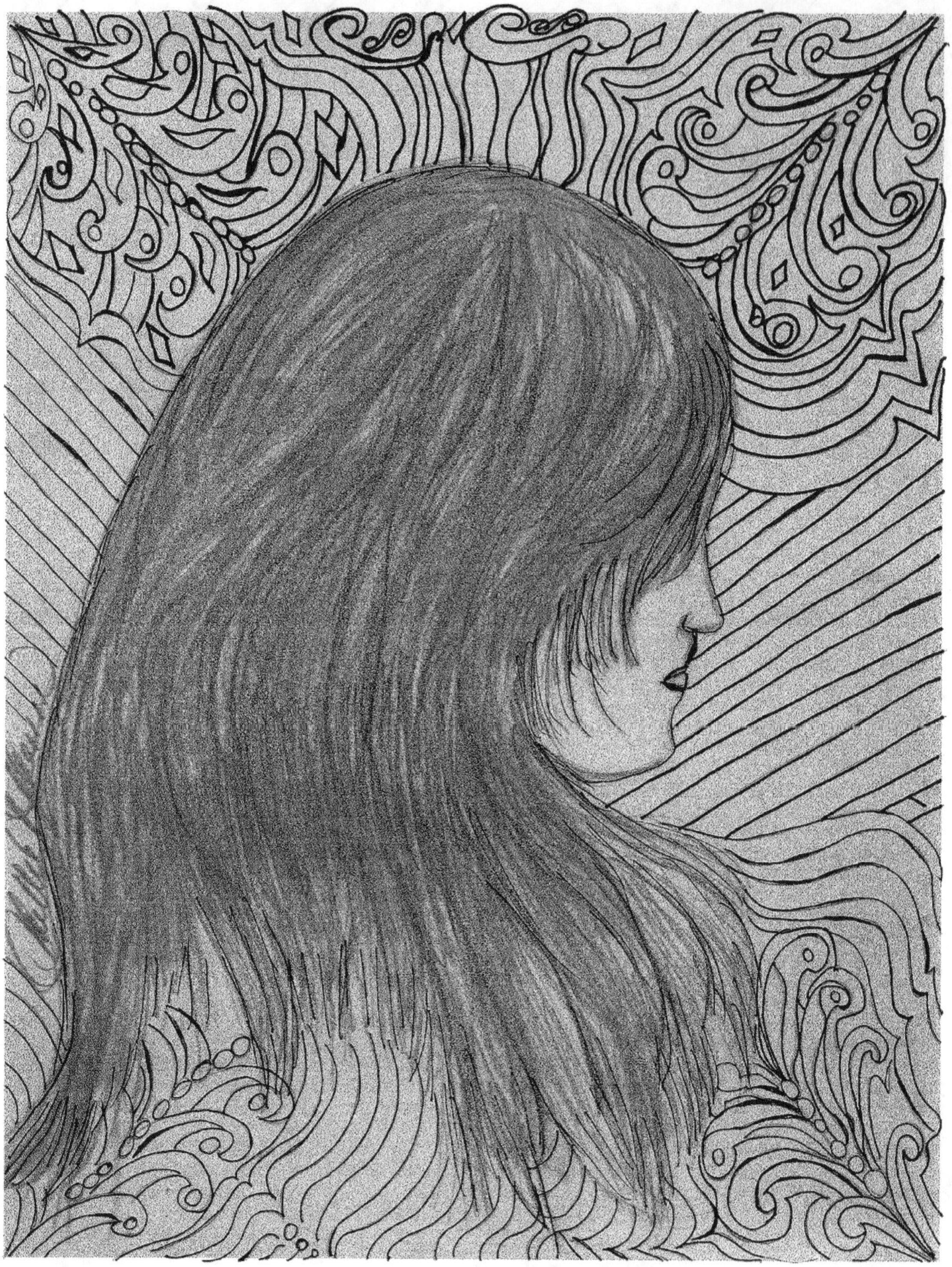

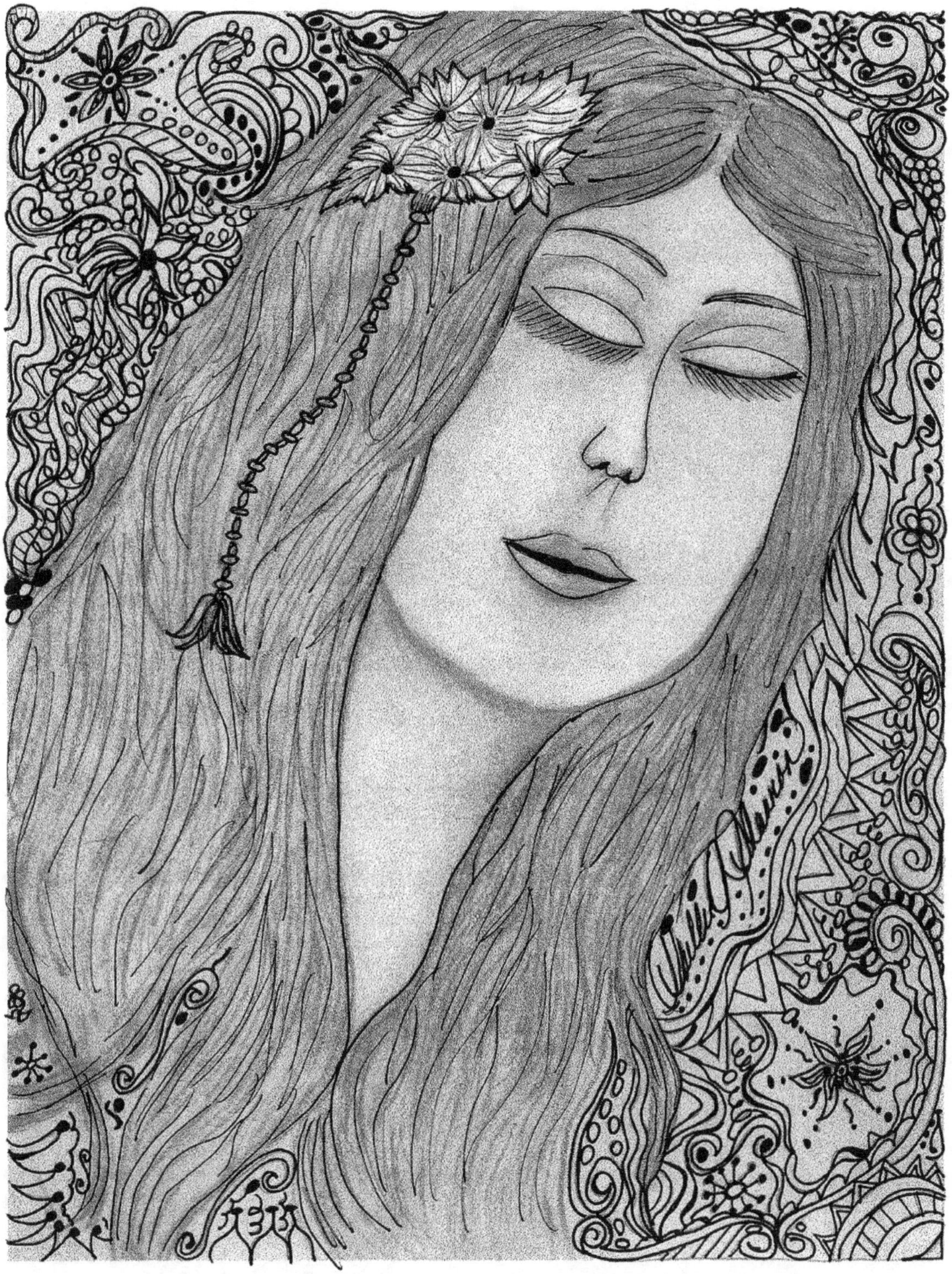

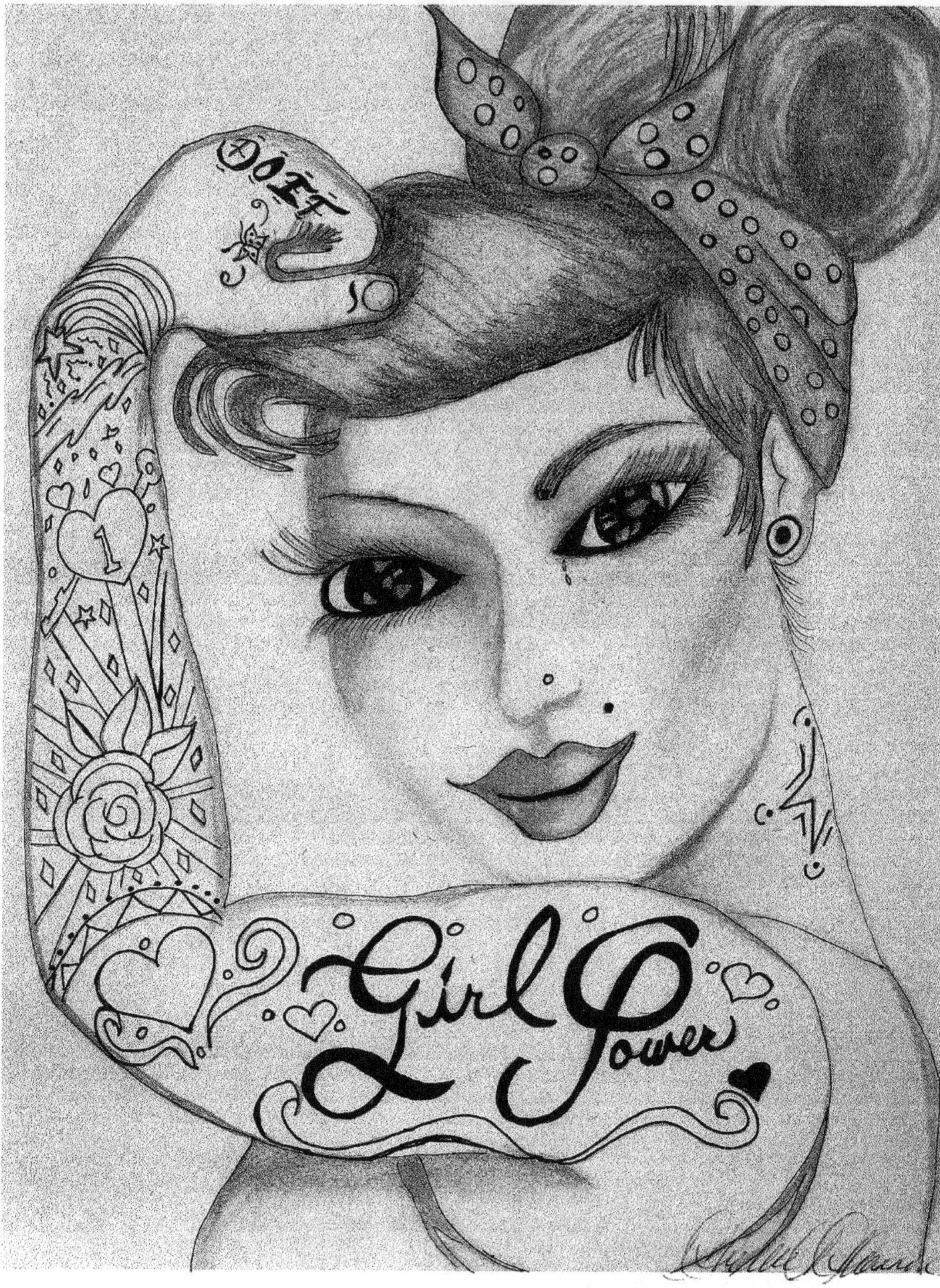
Girl Power

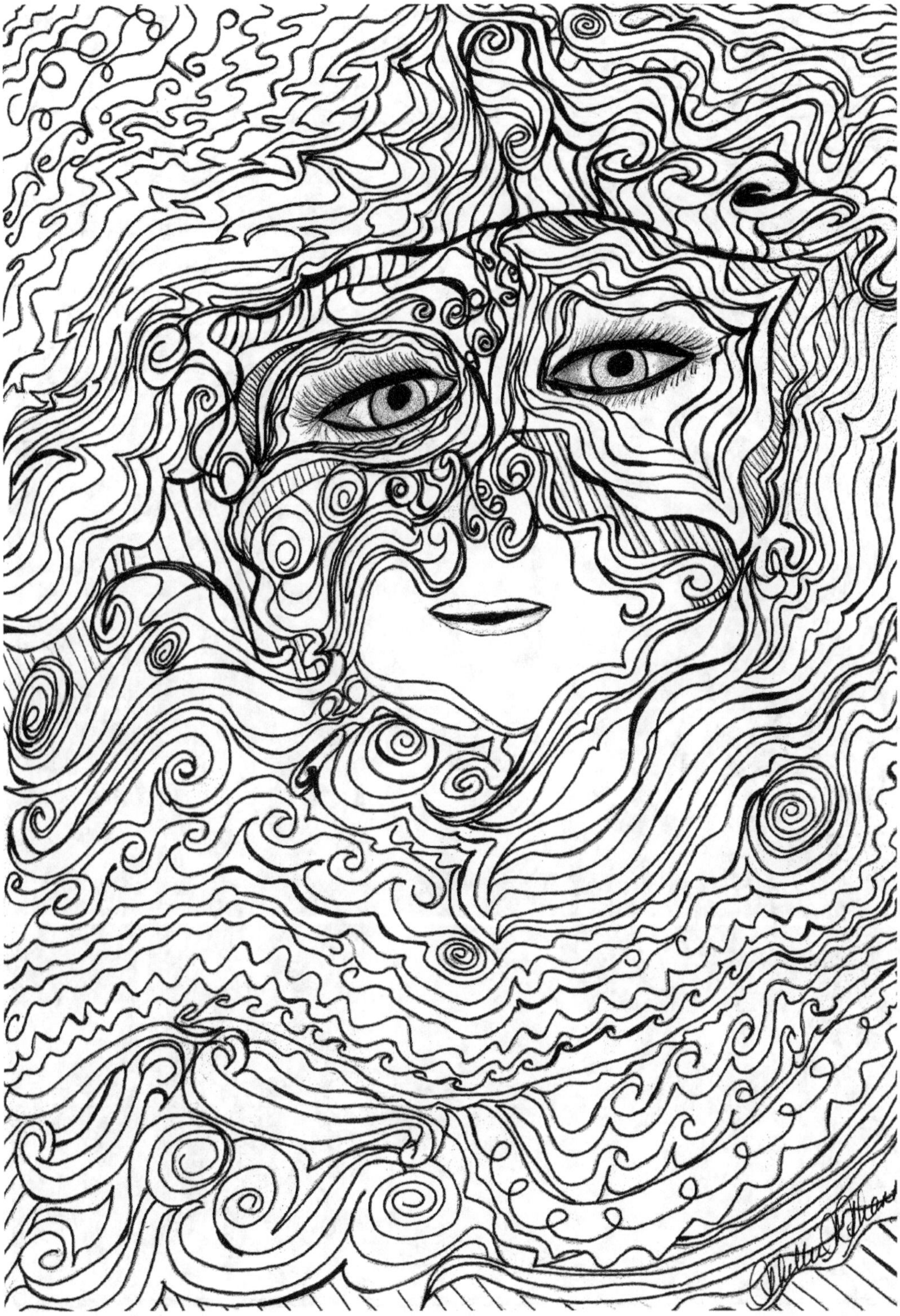

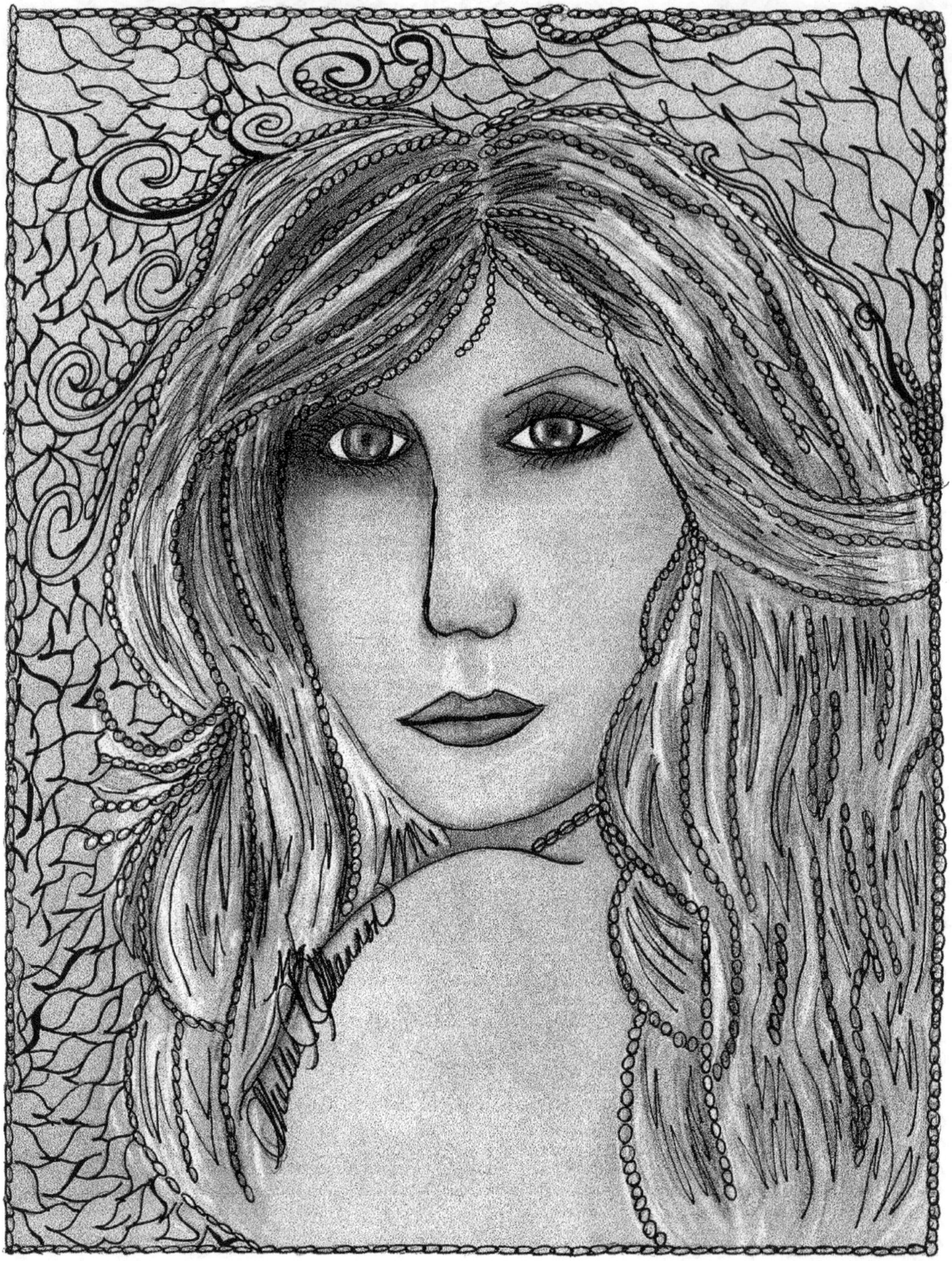

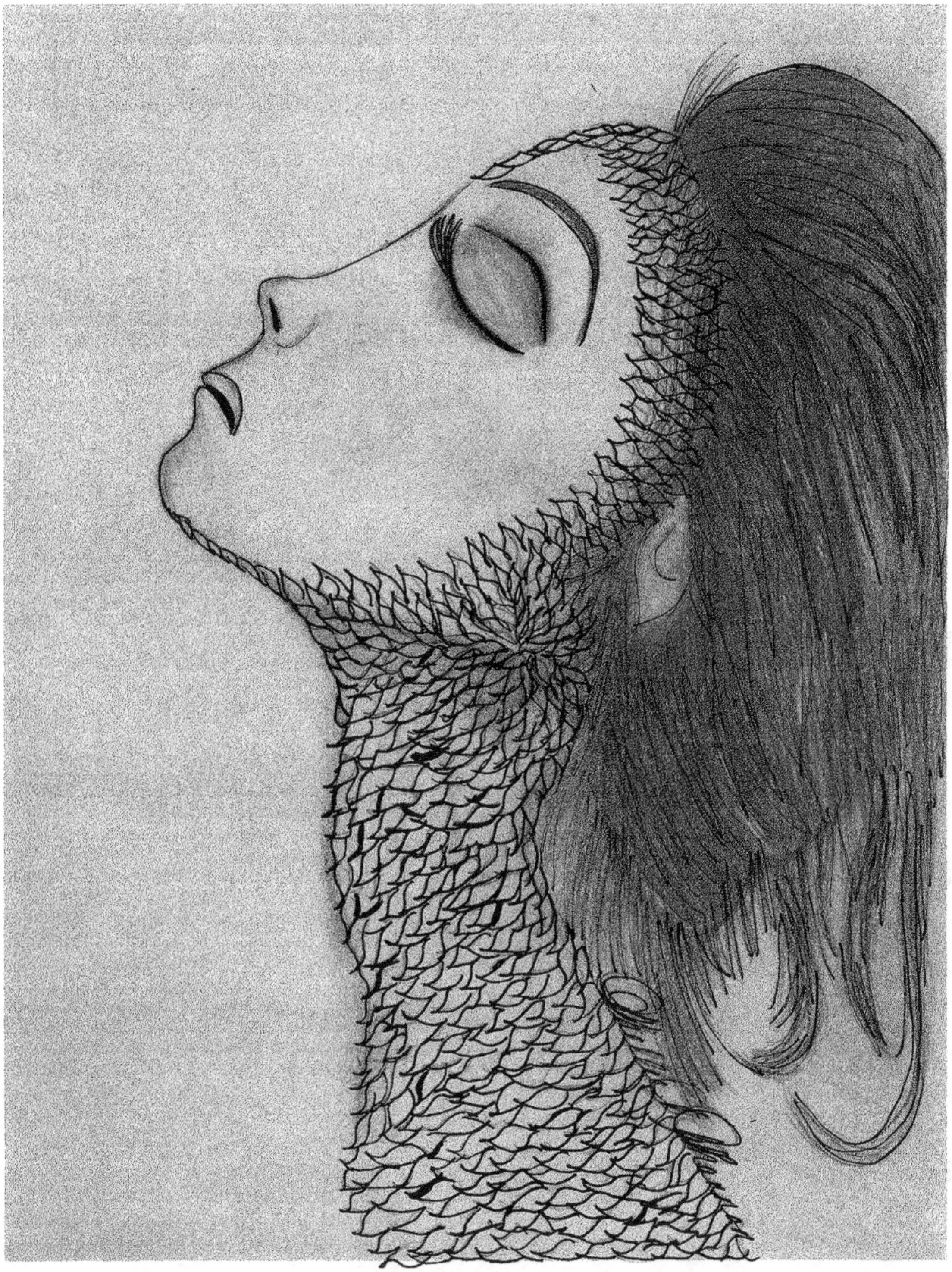

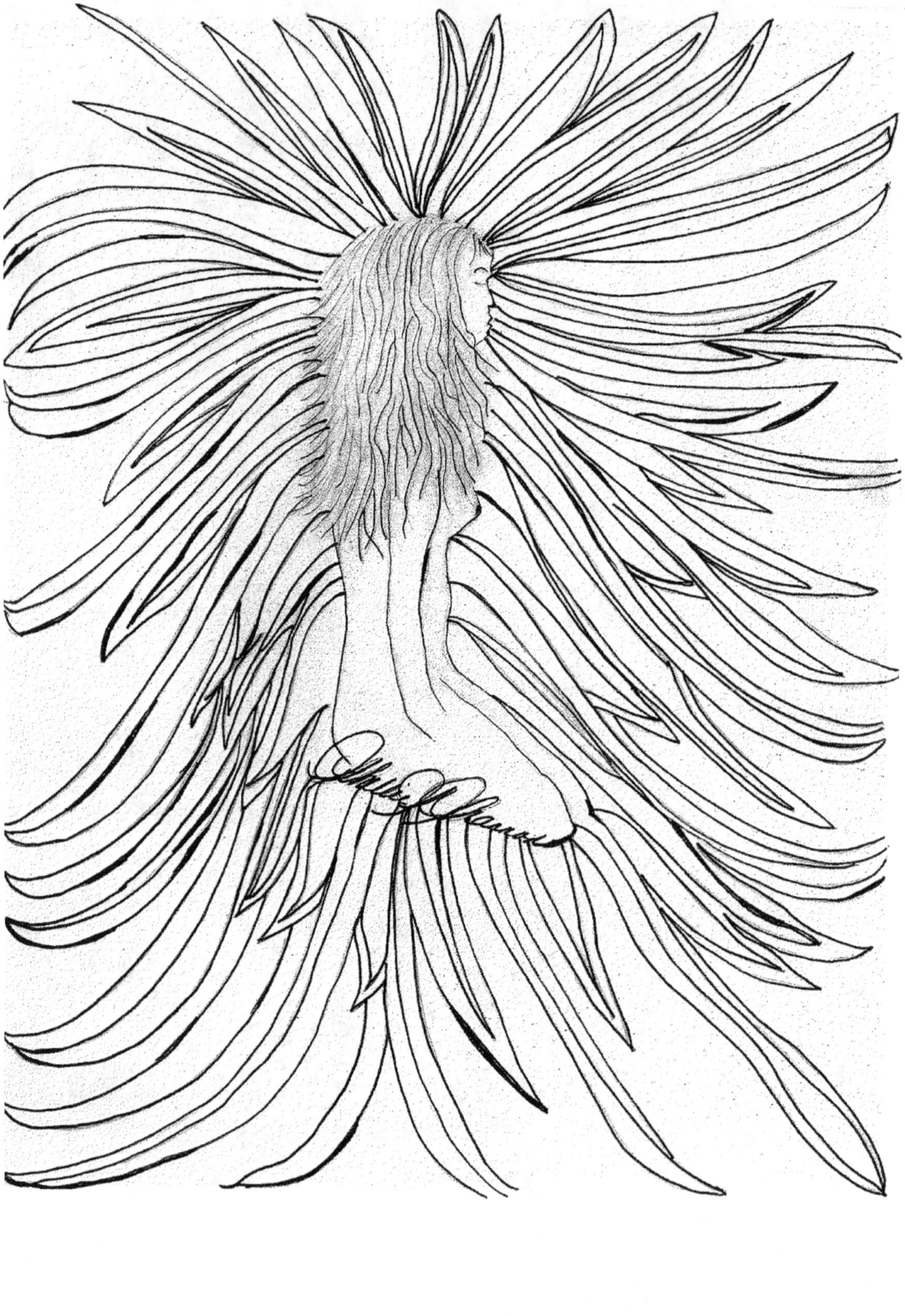

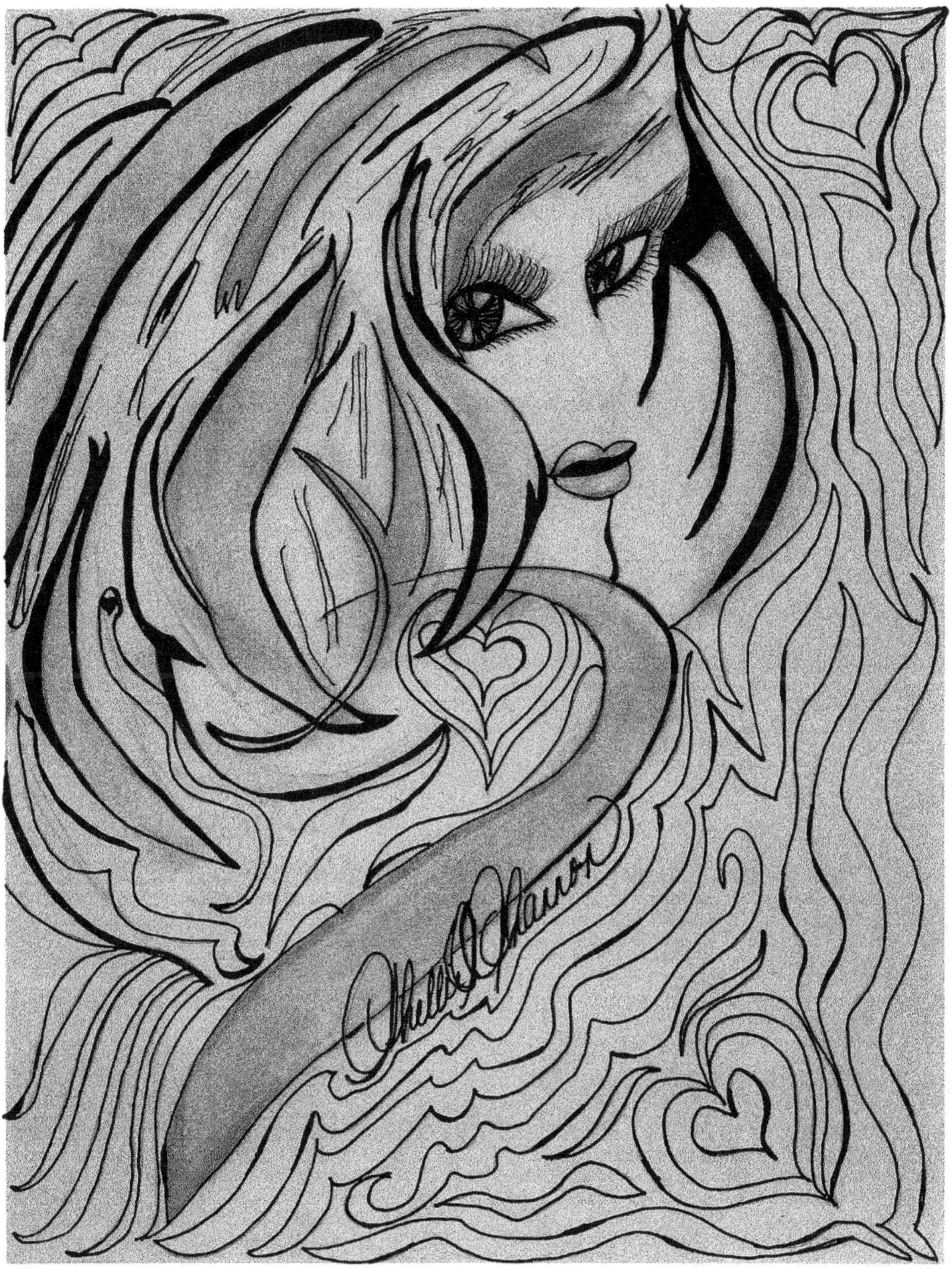

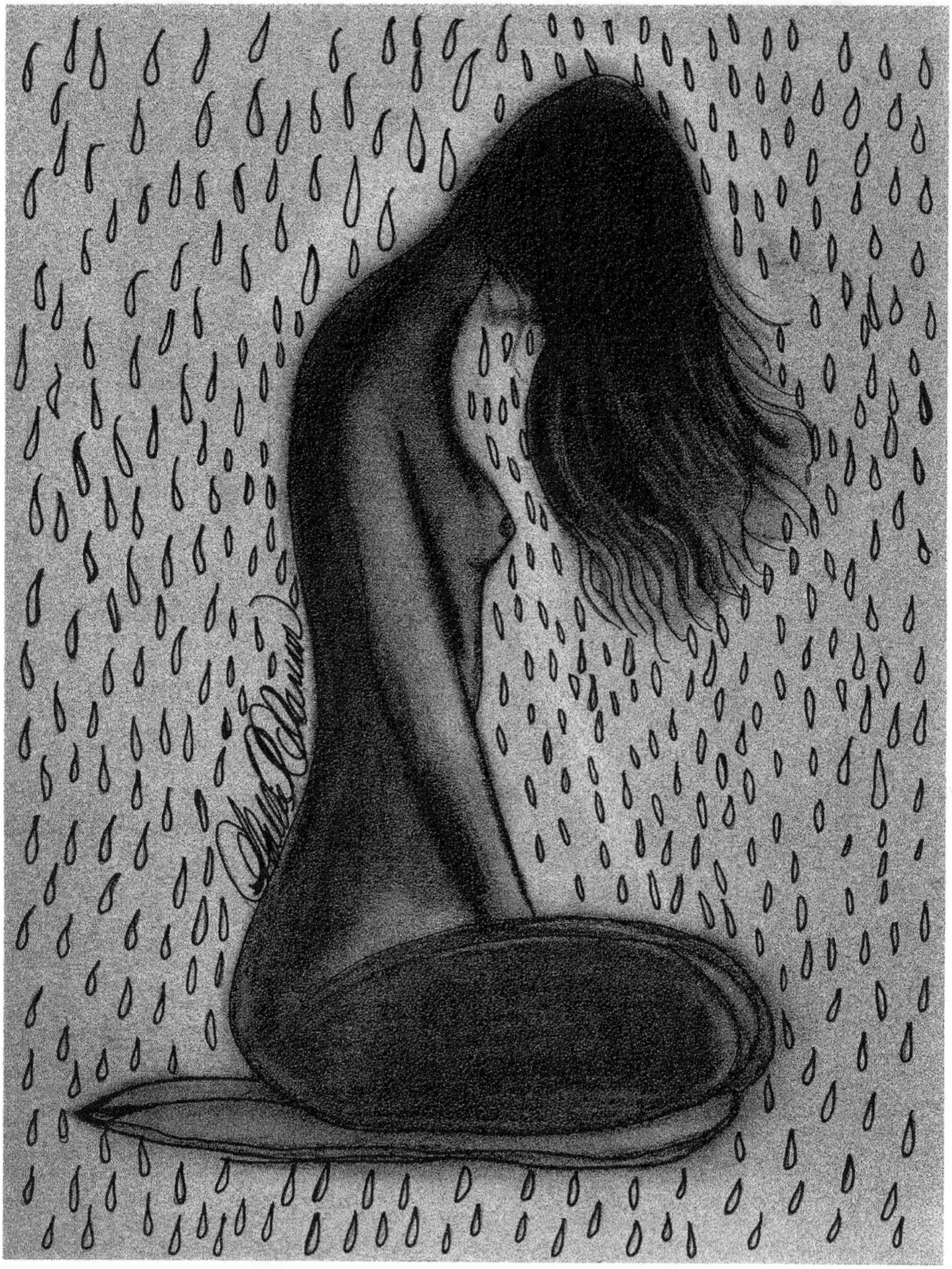

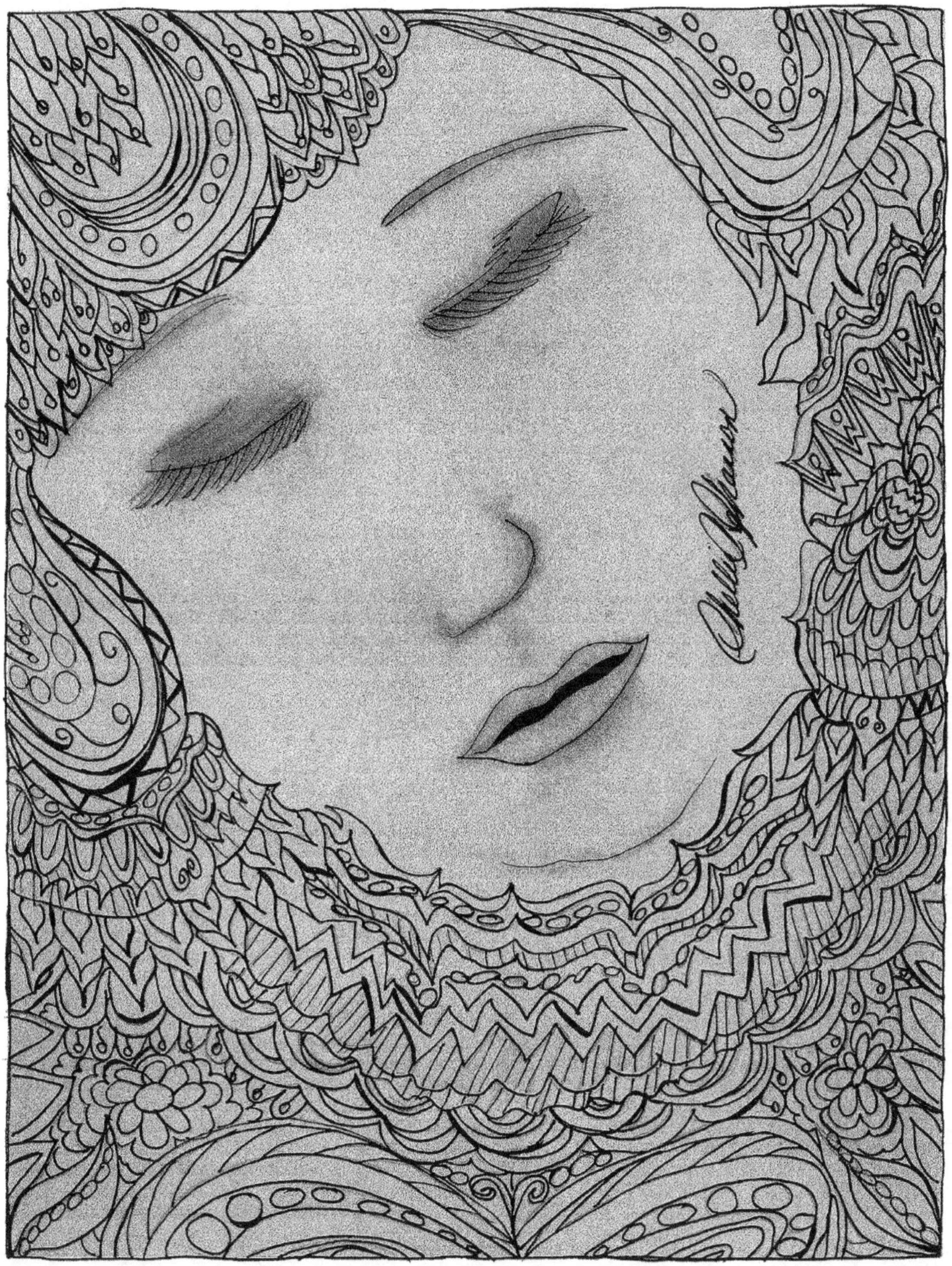

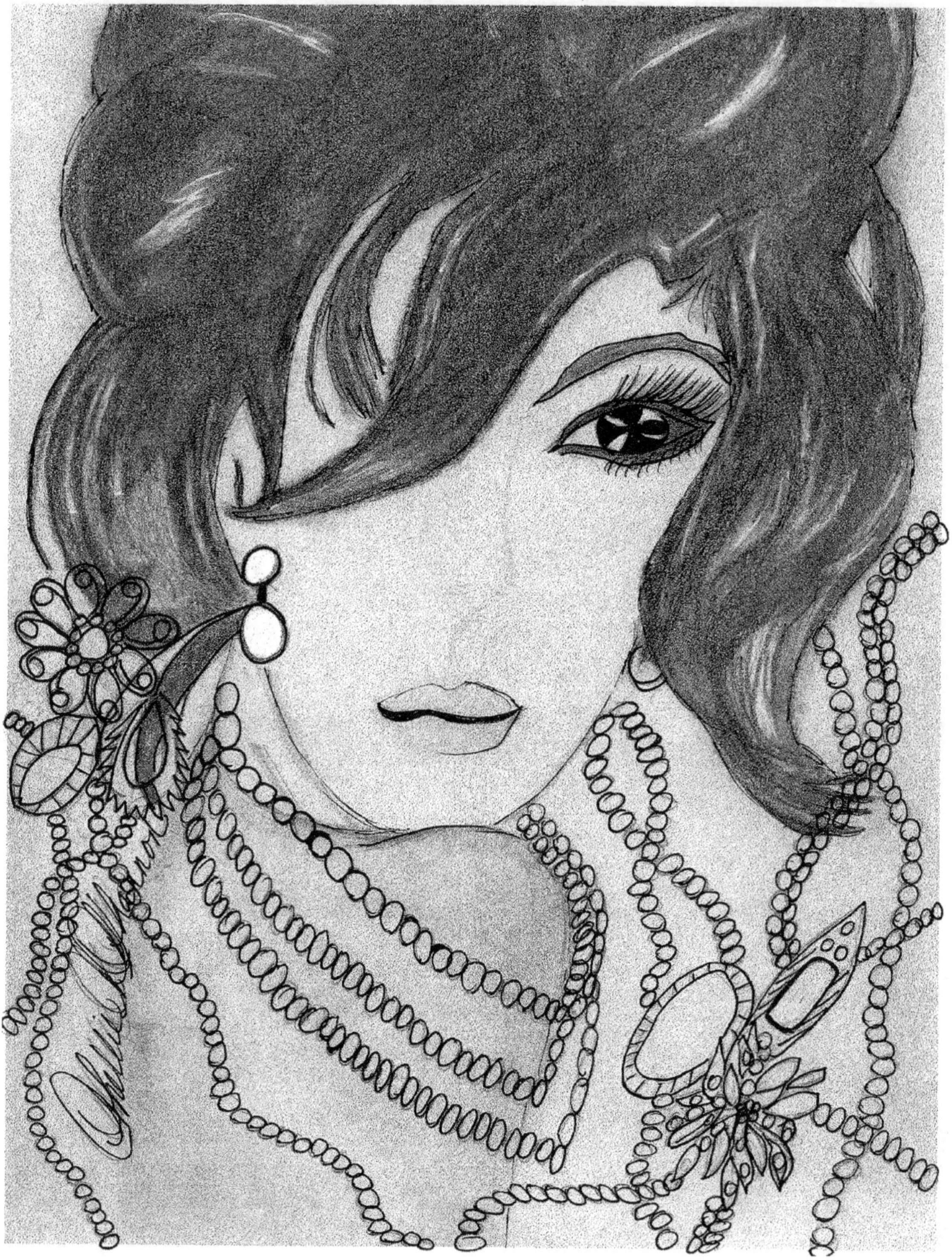

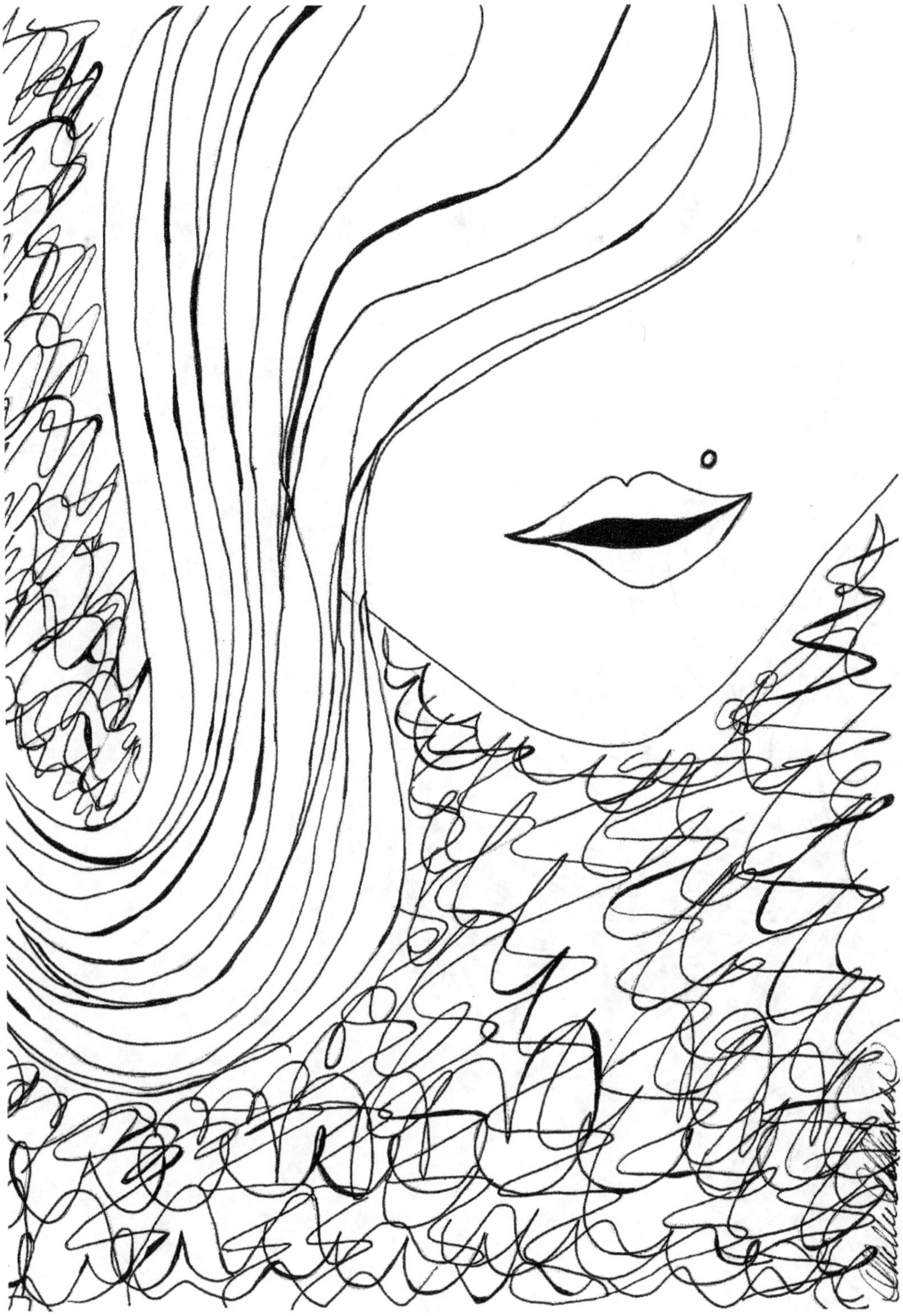

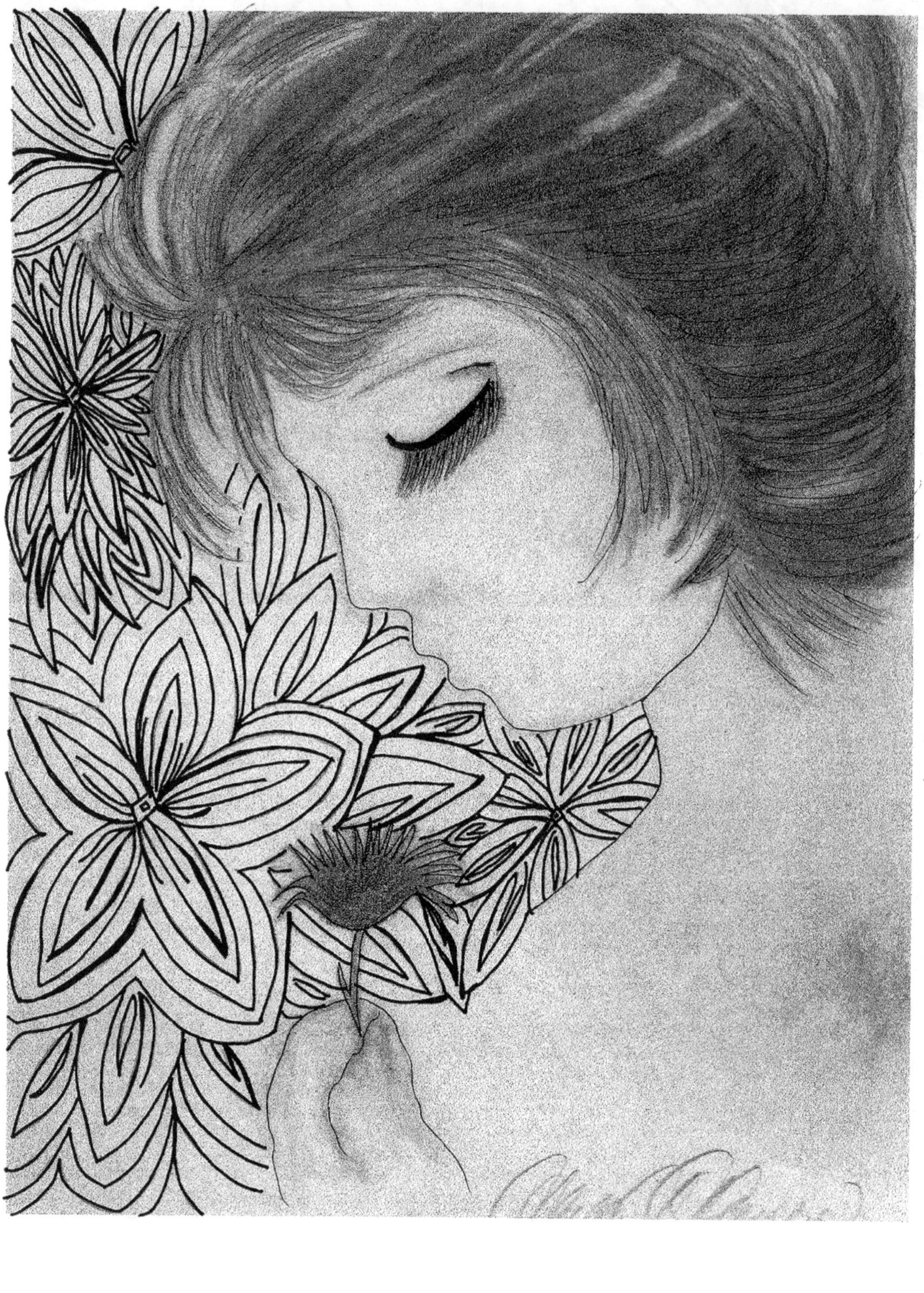

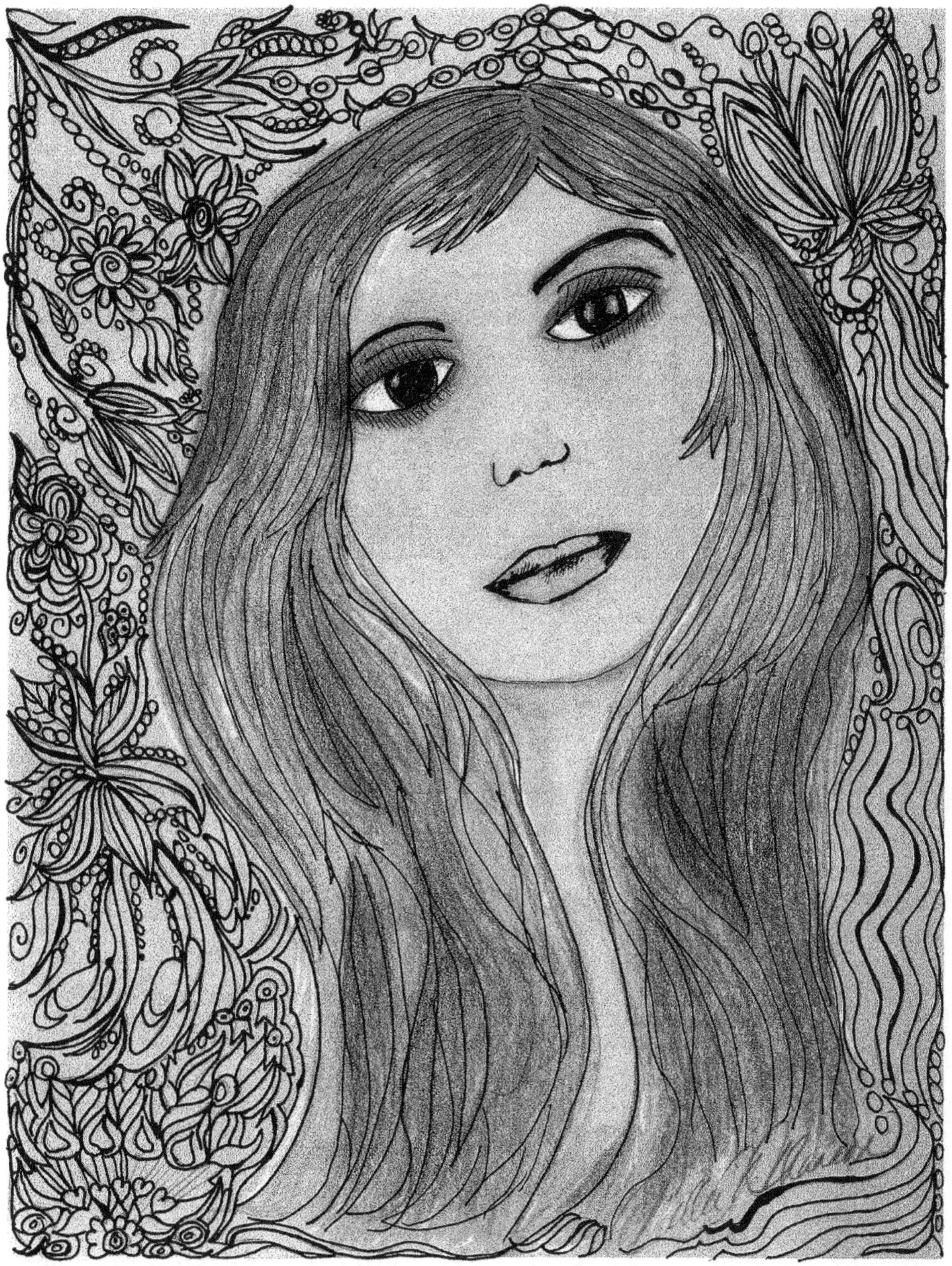

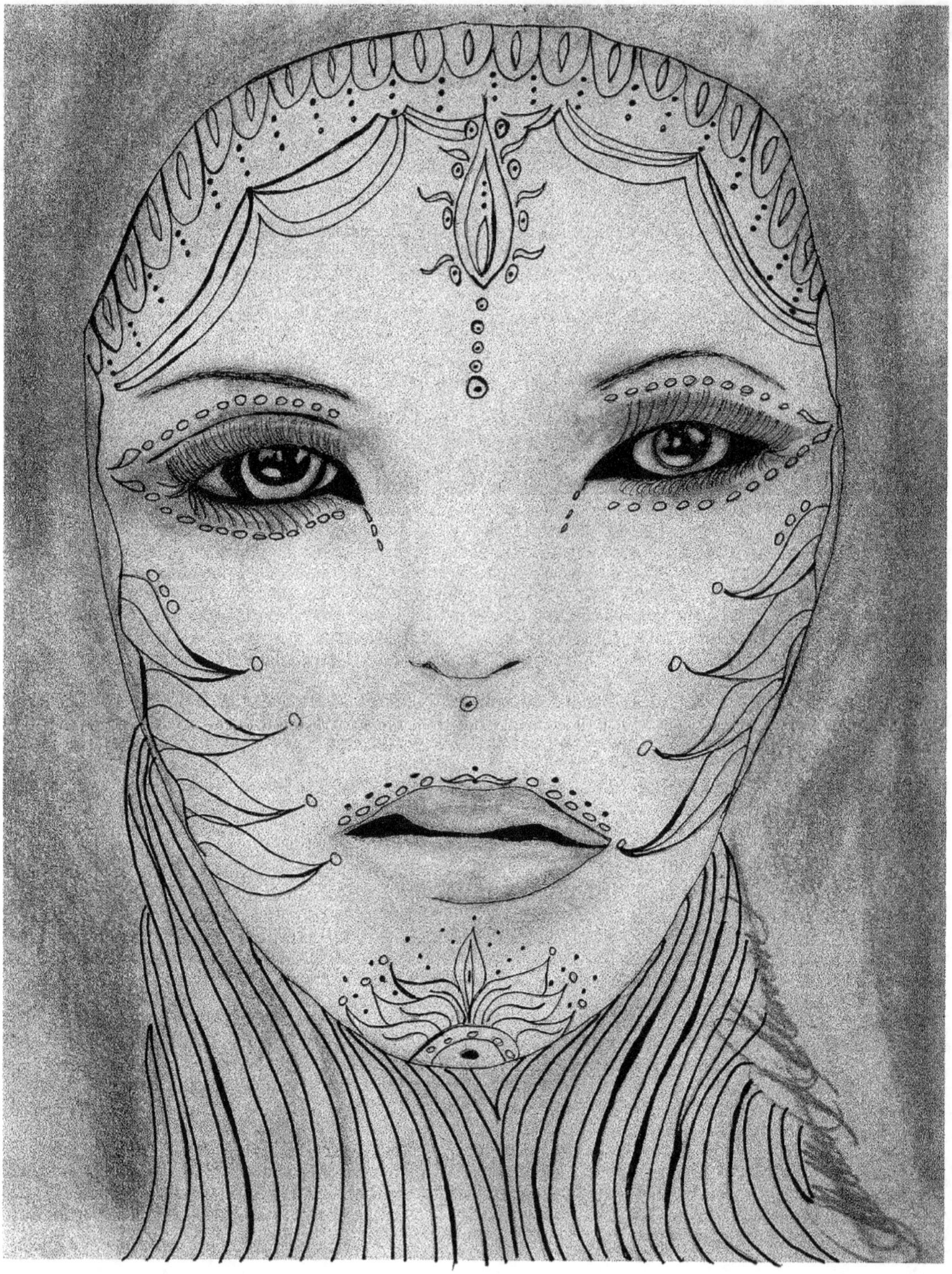

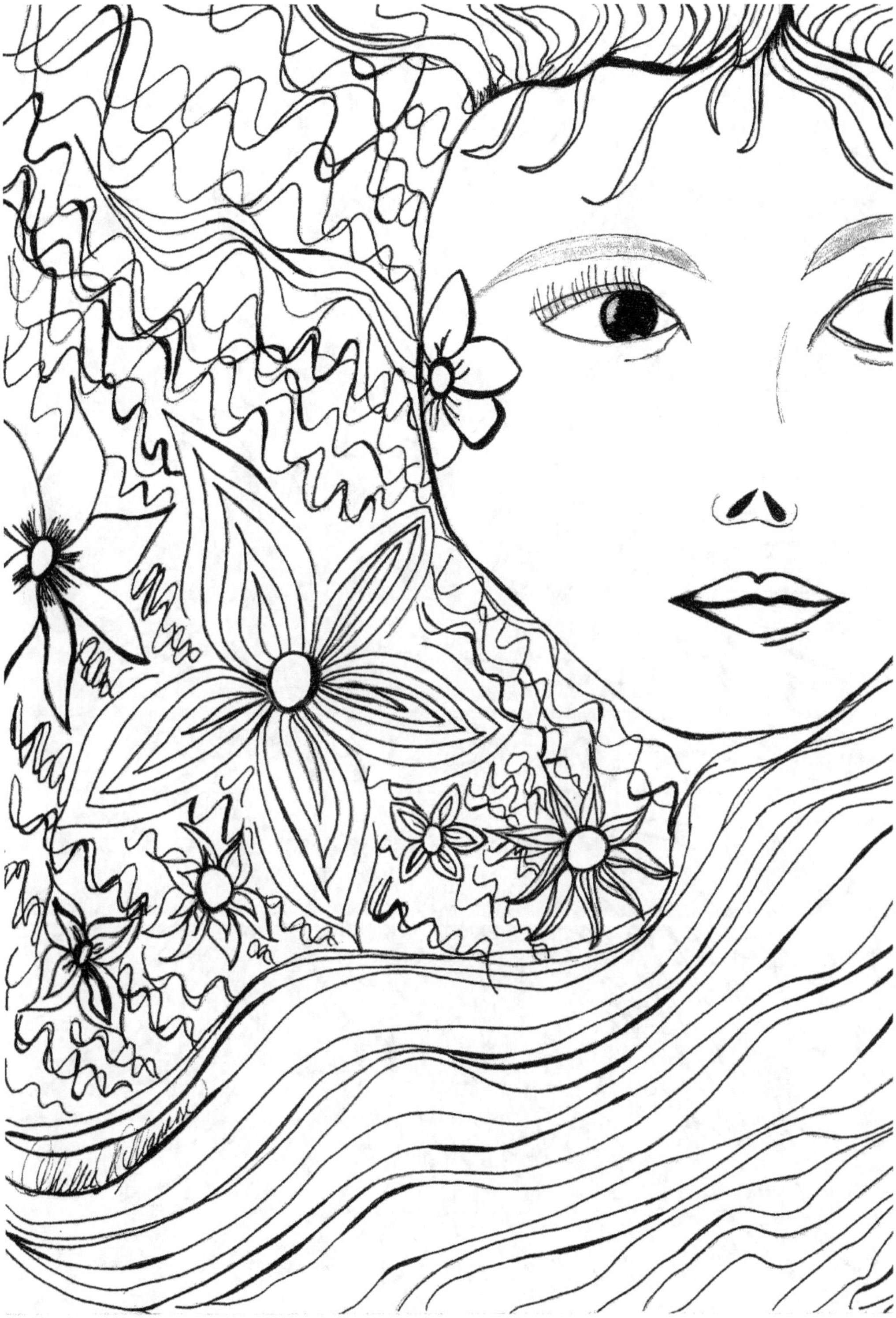

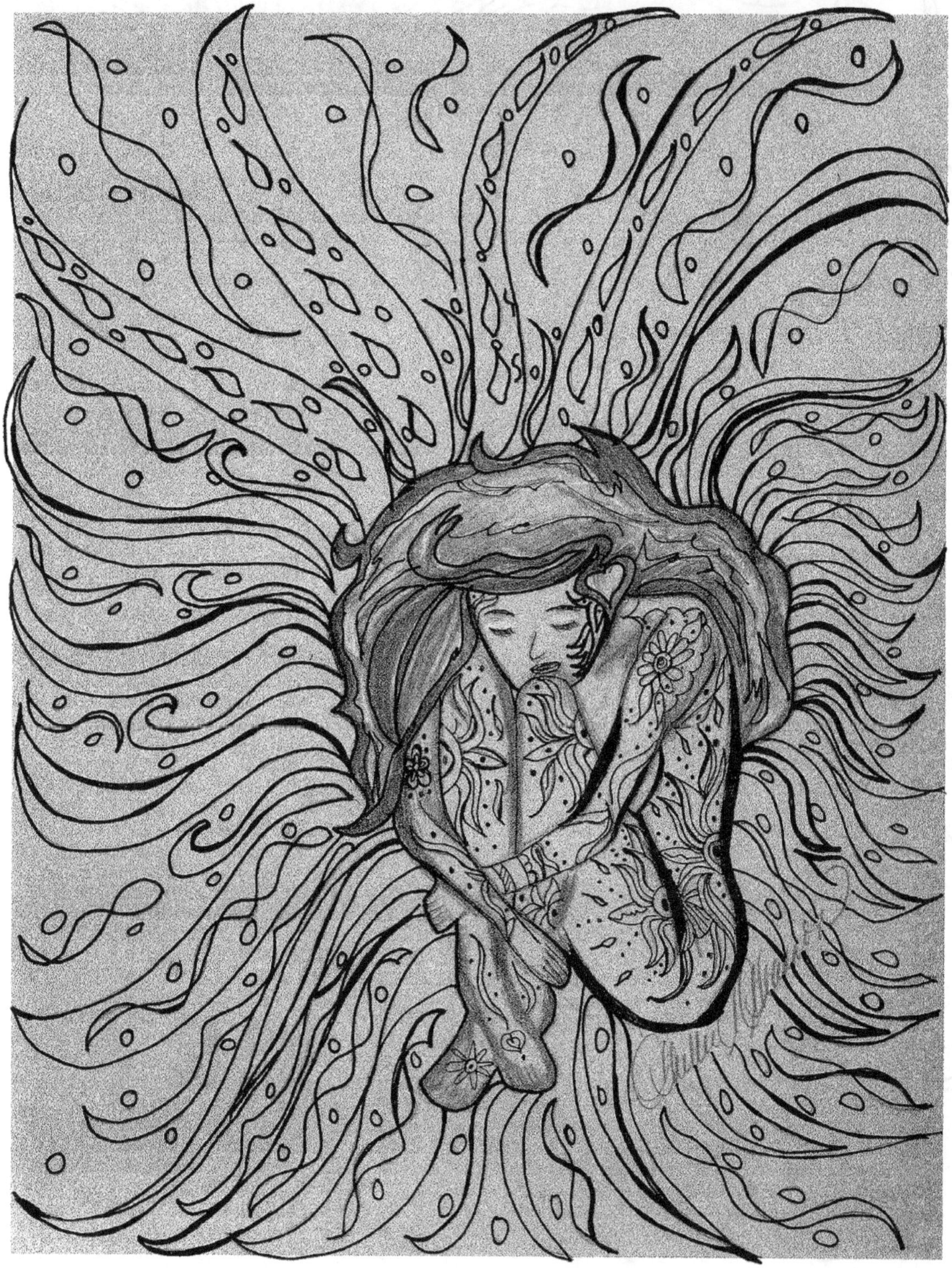

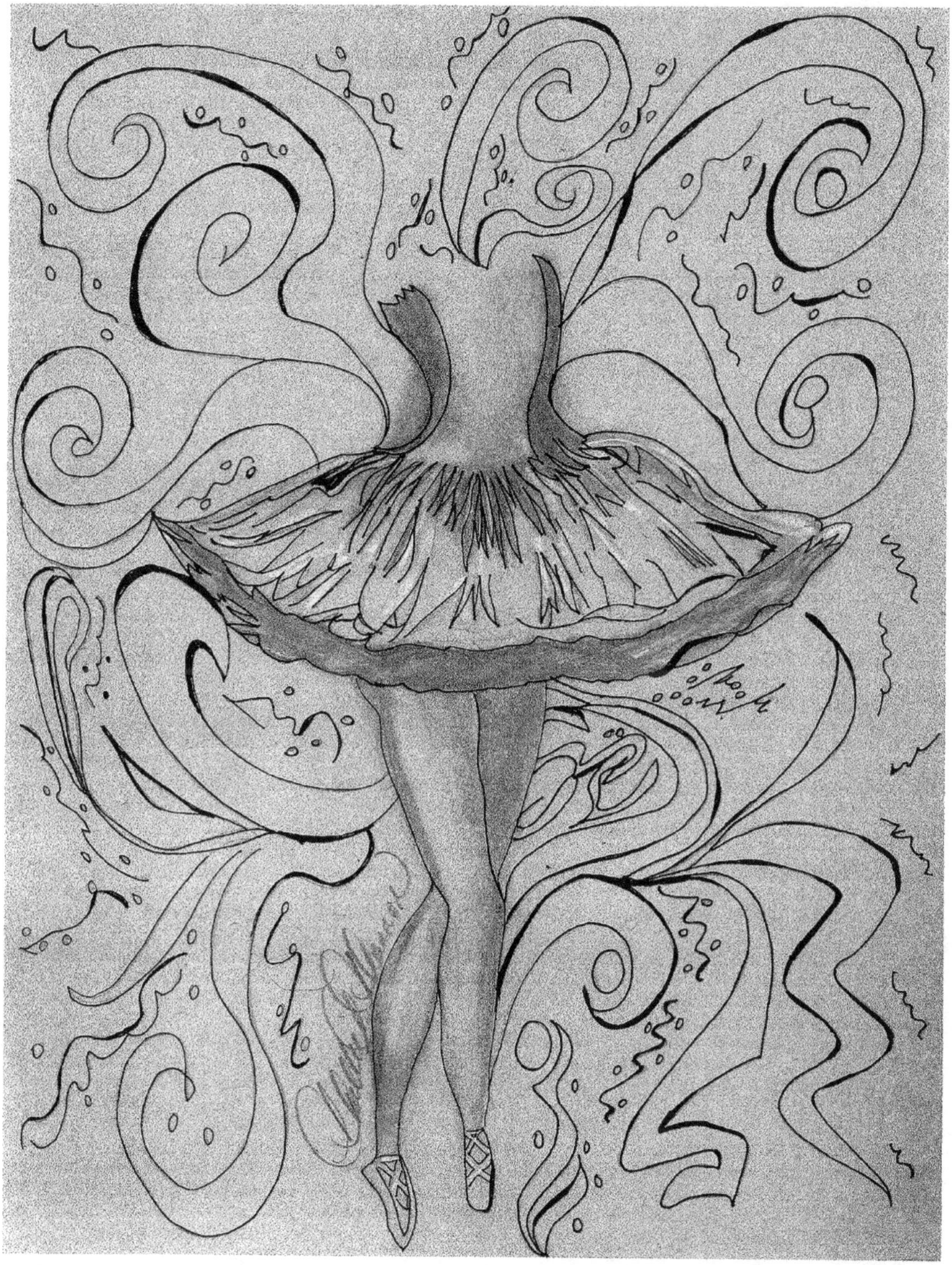

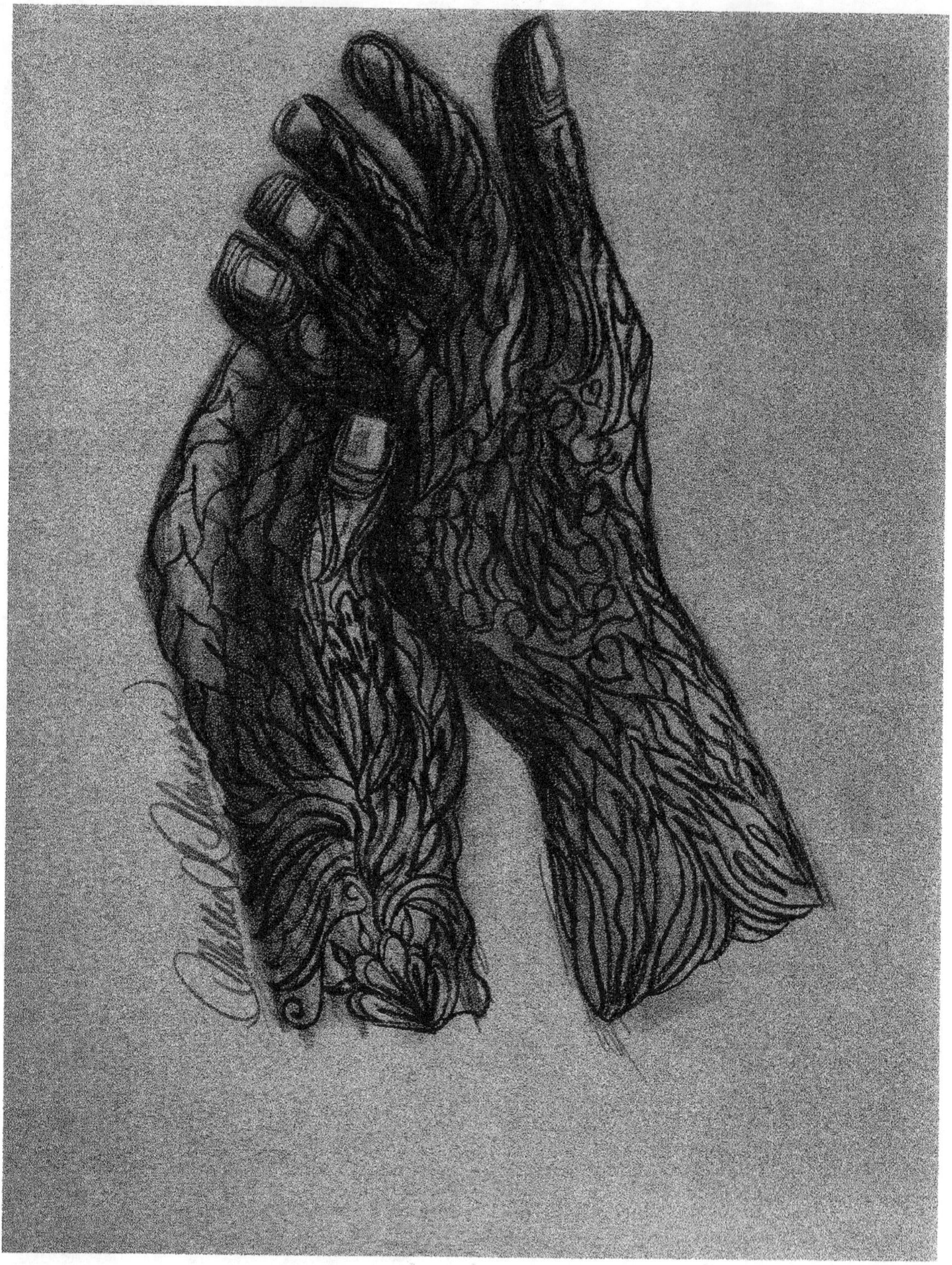

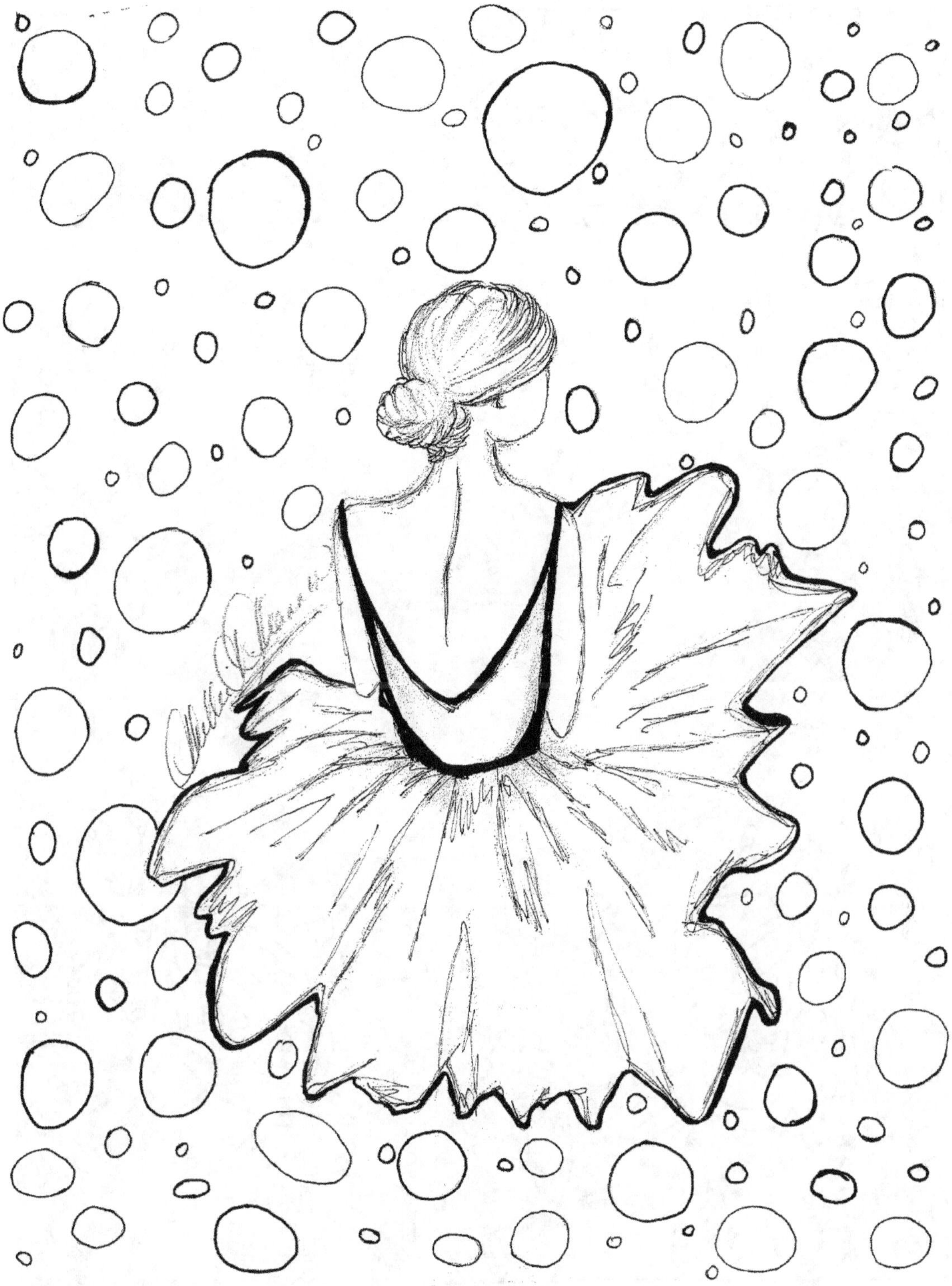

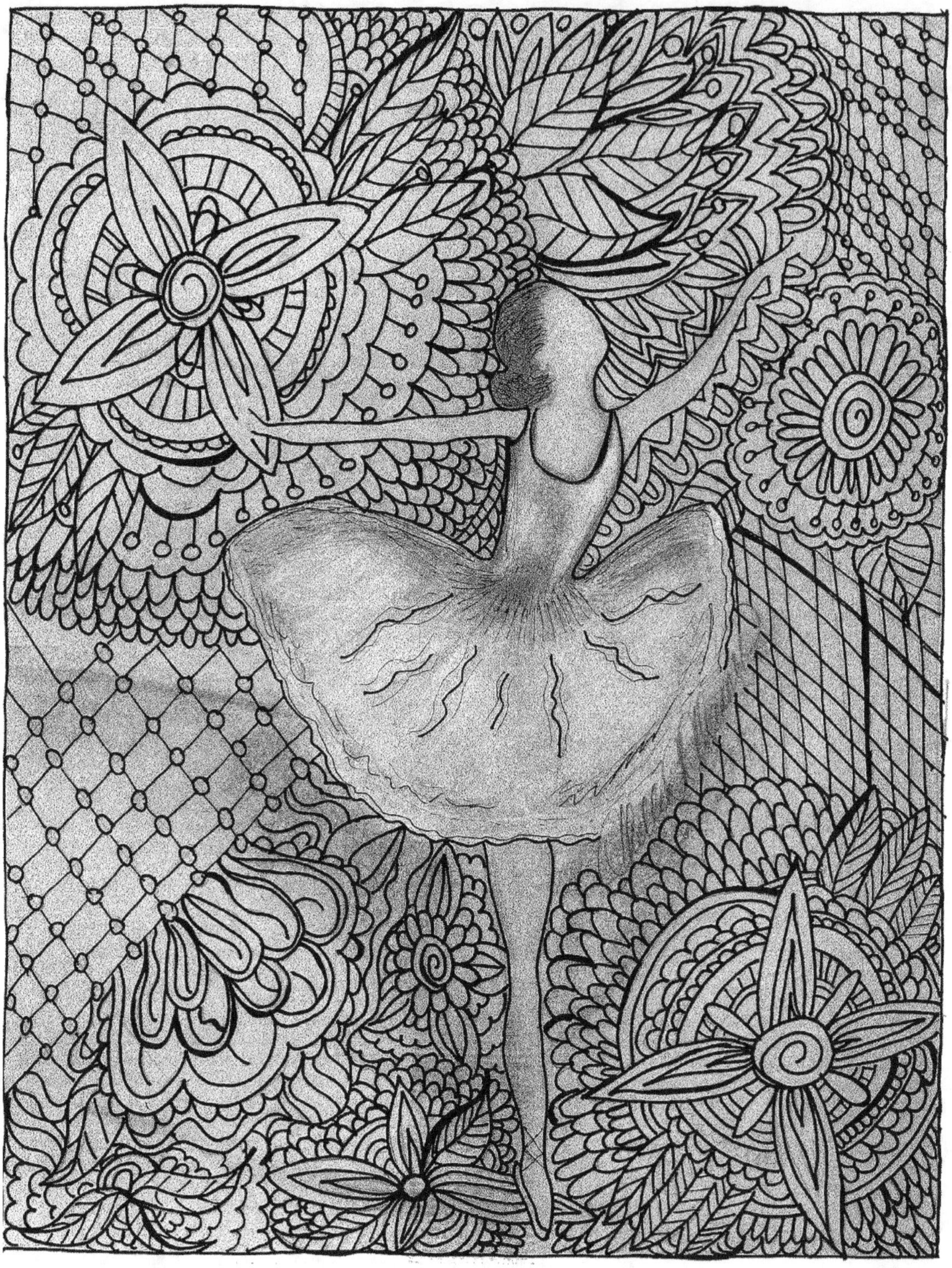

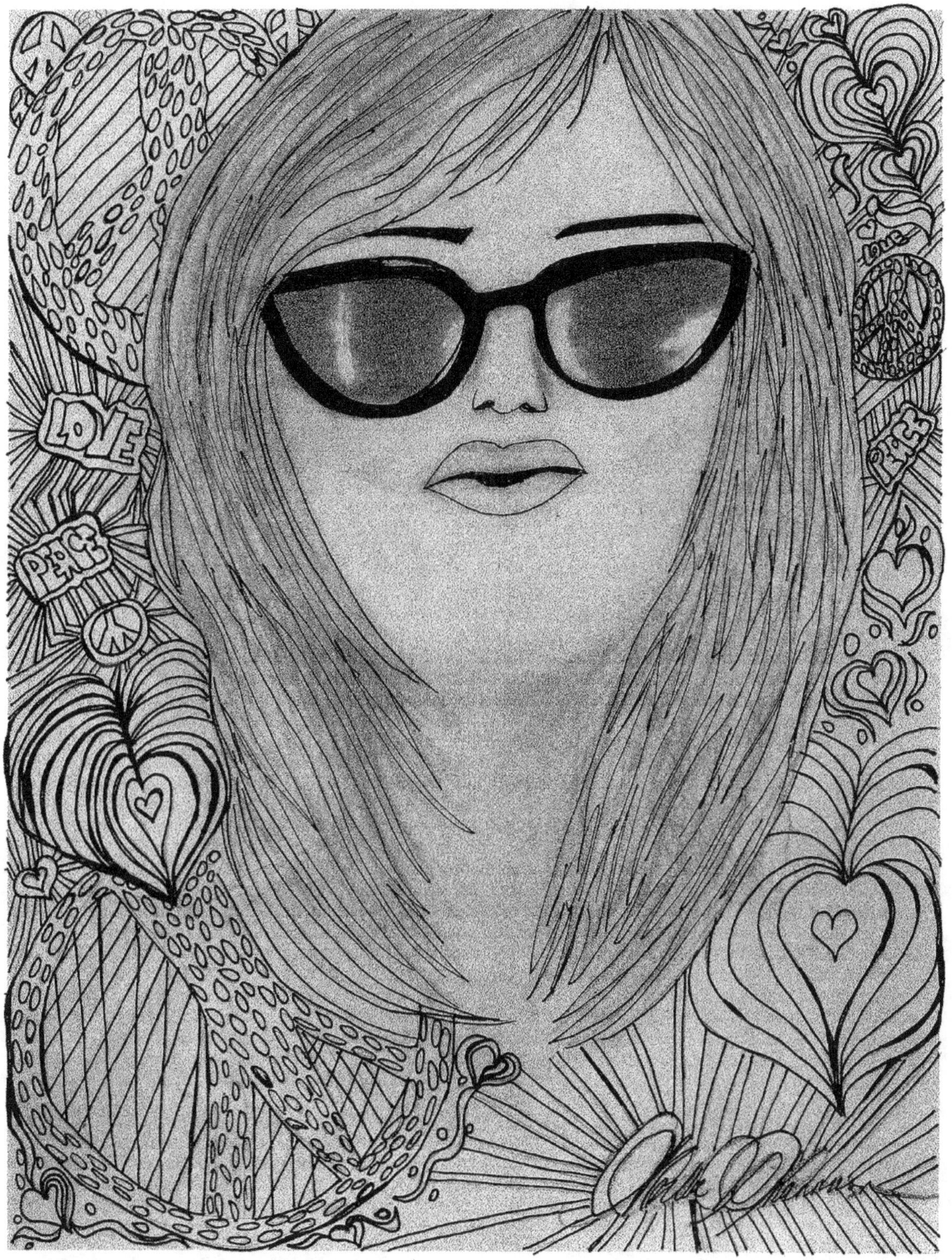
LOVE
PEACE

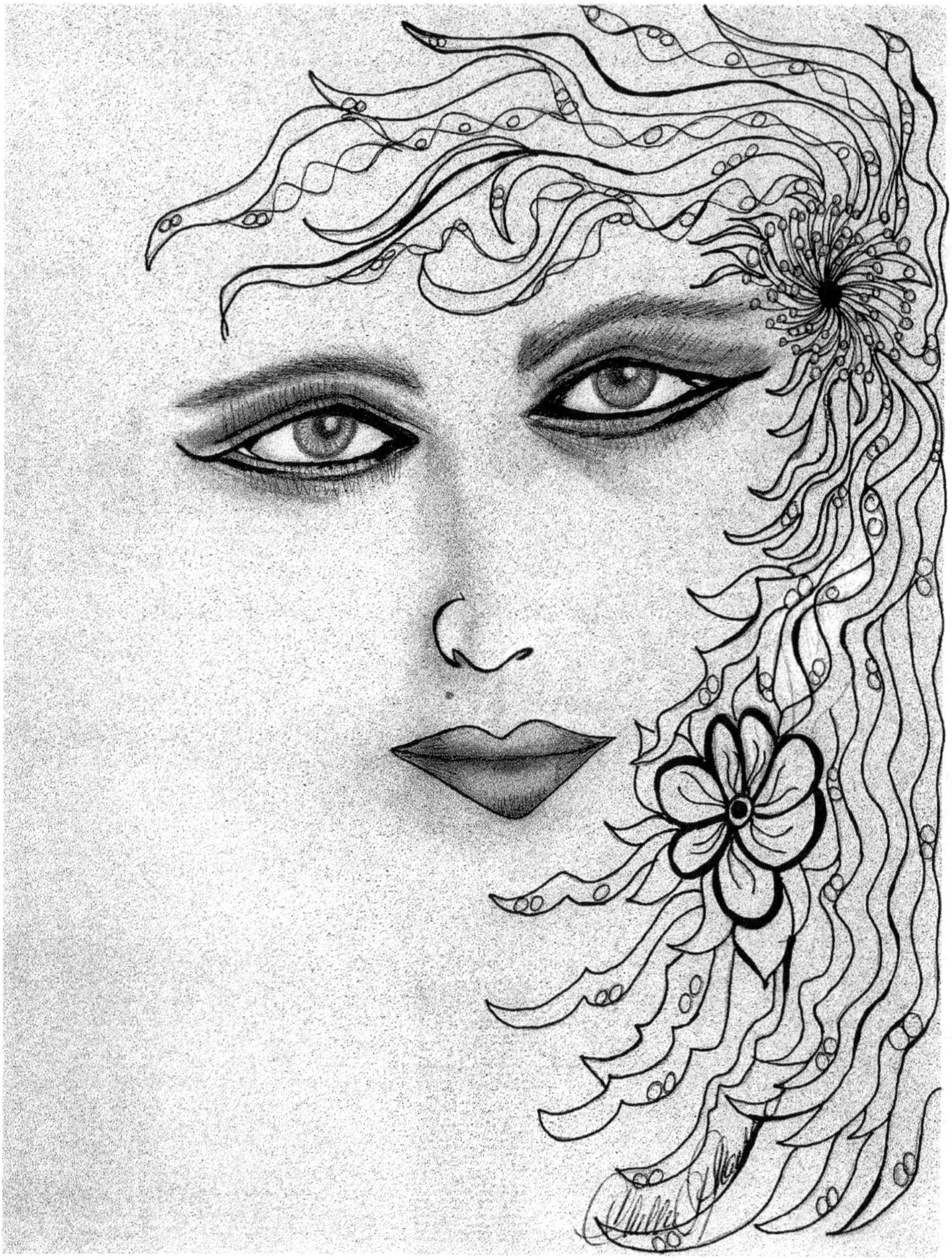

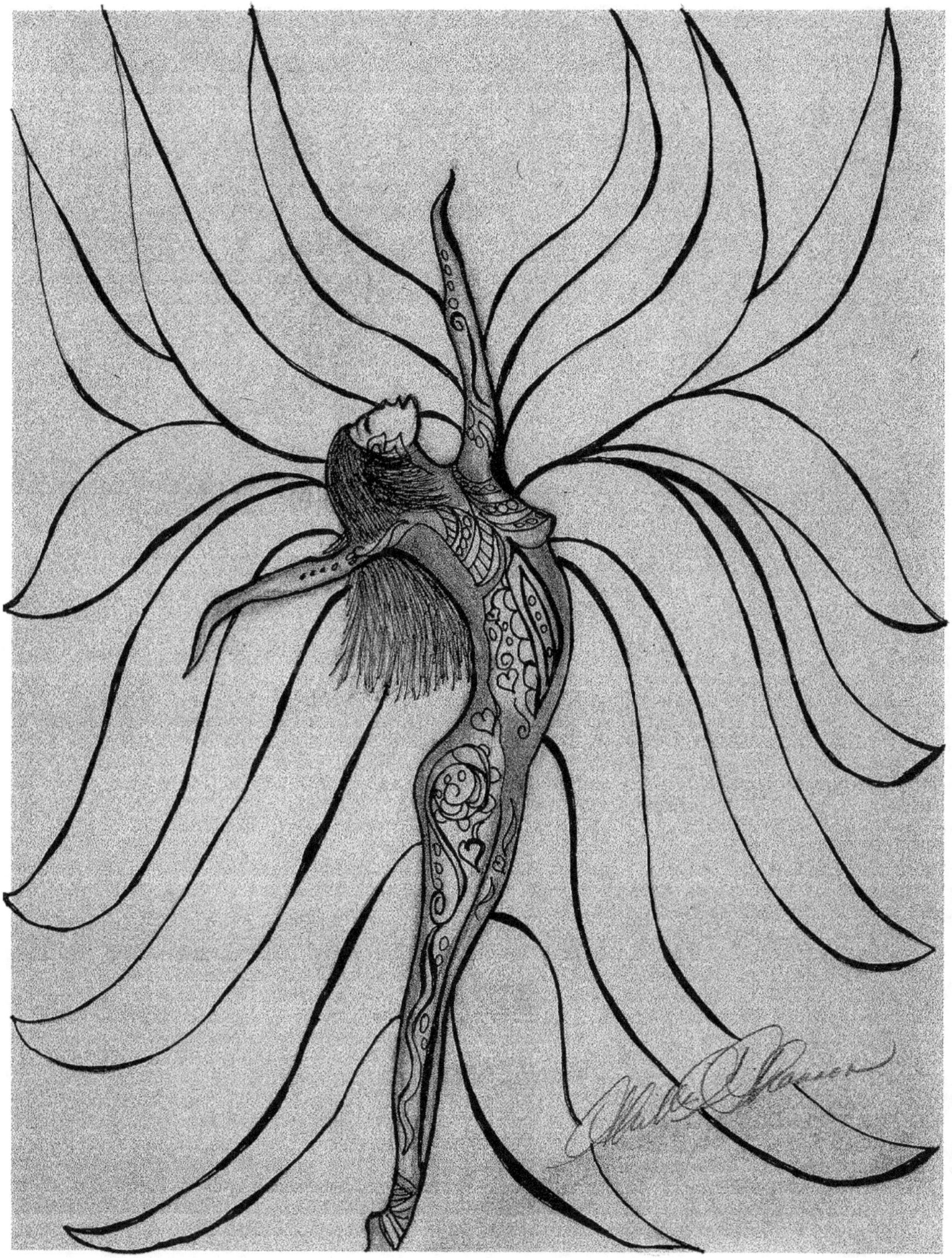

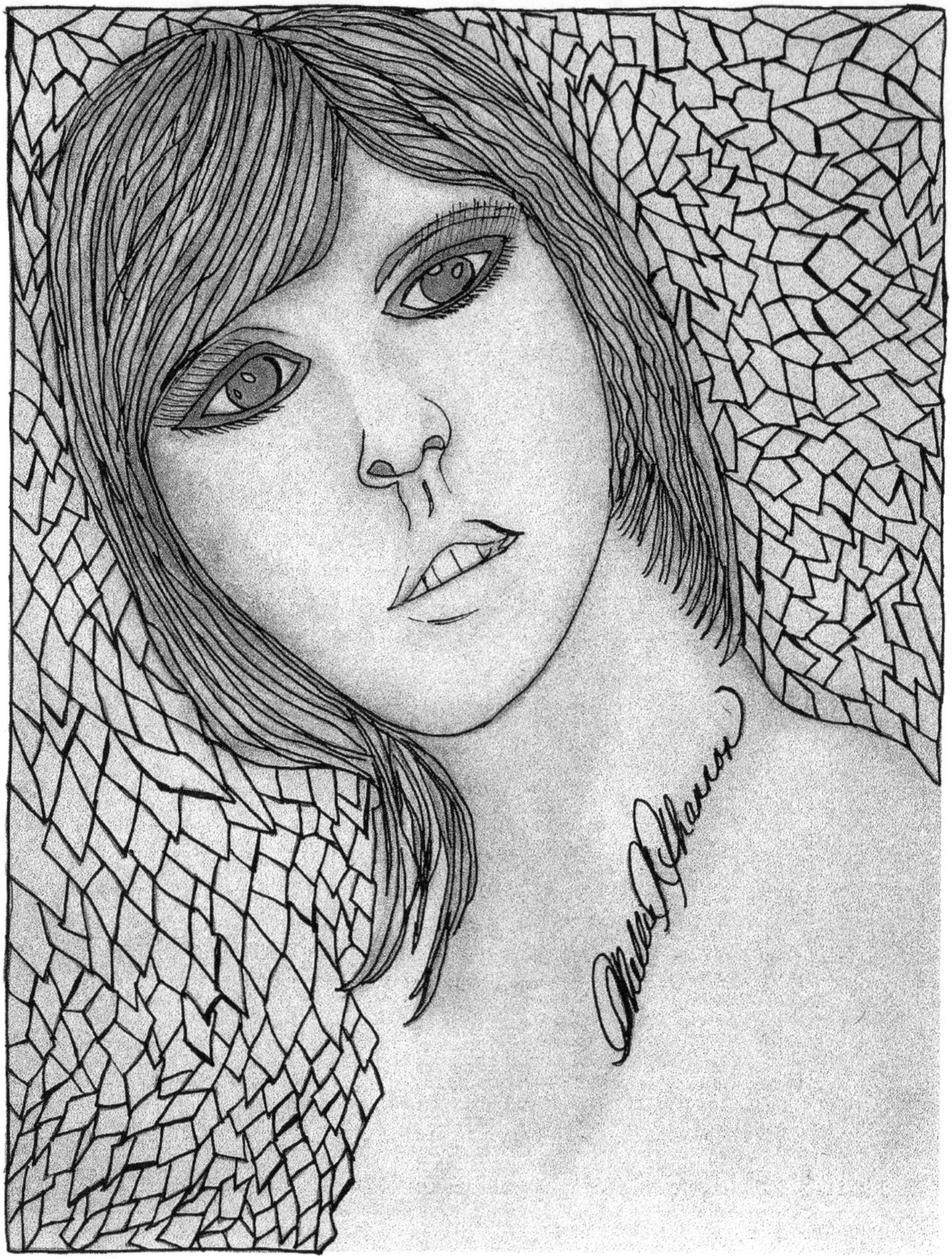

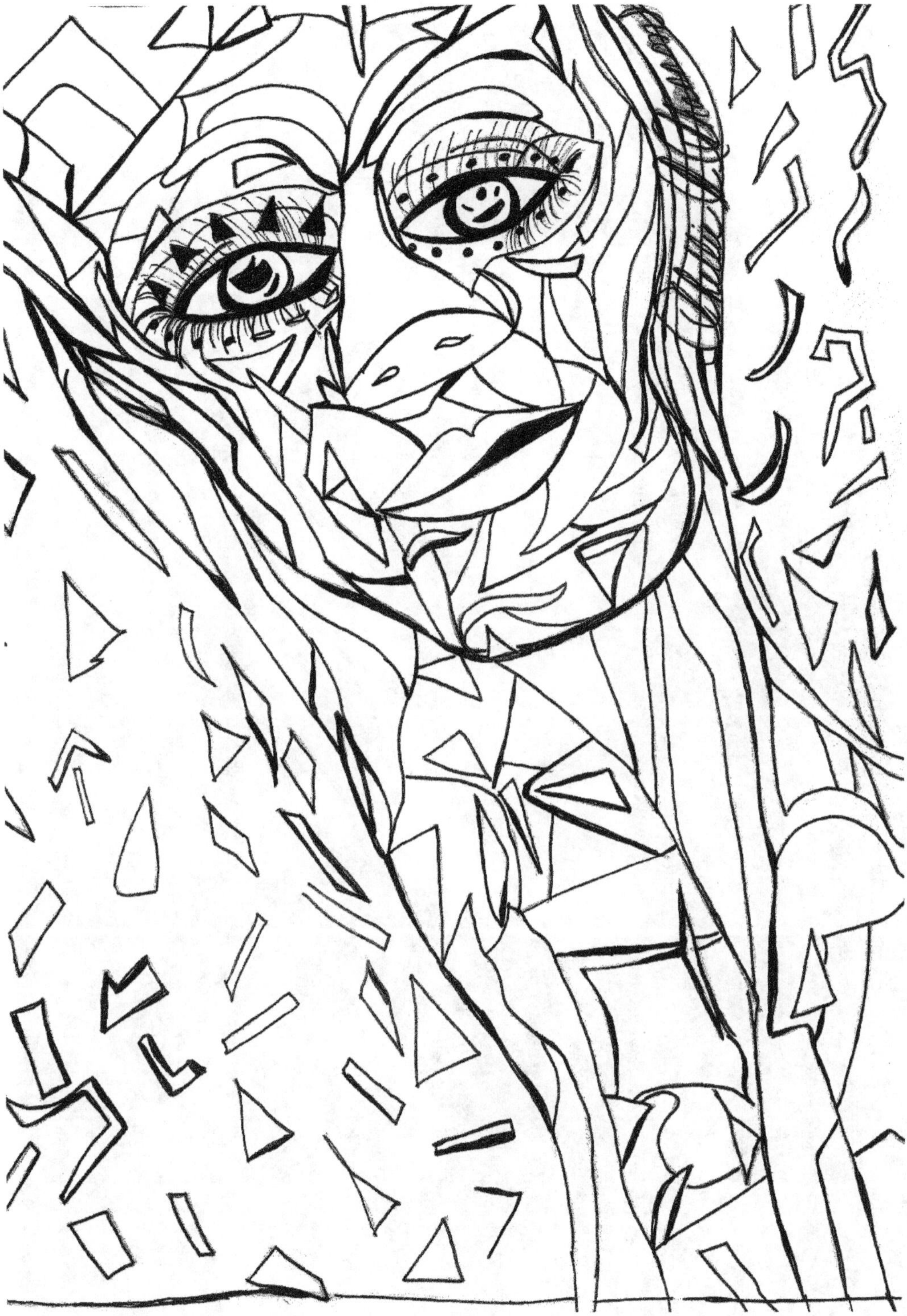

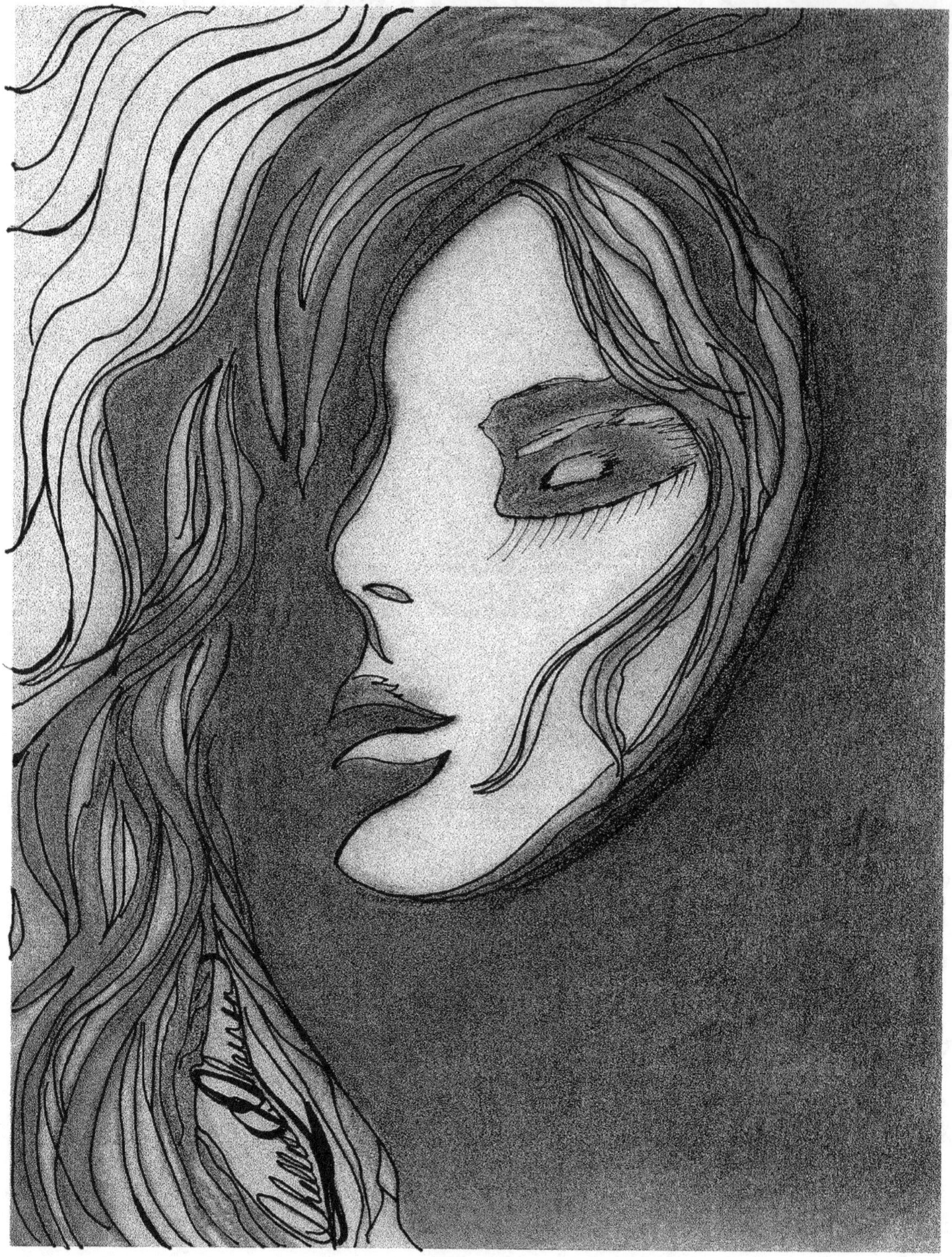

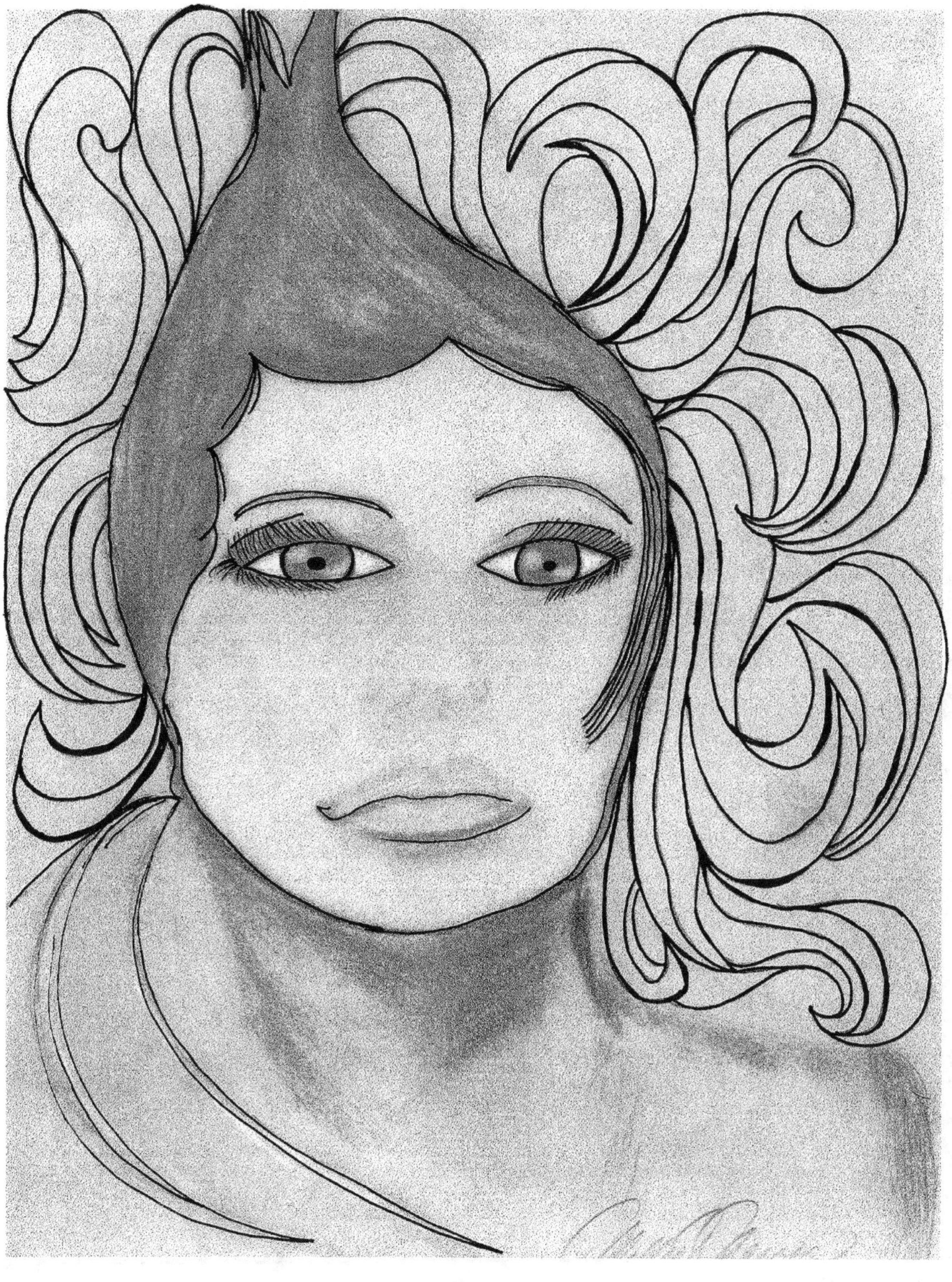

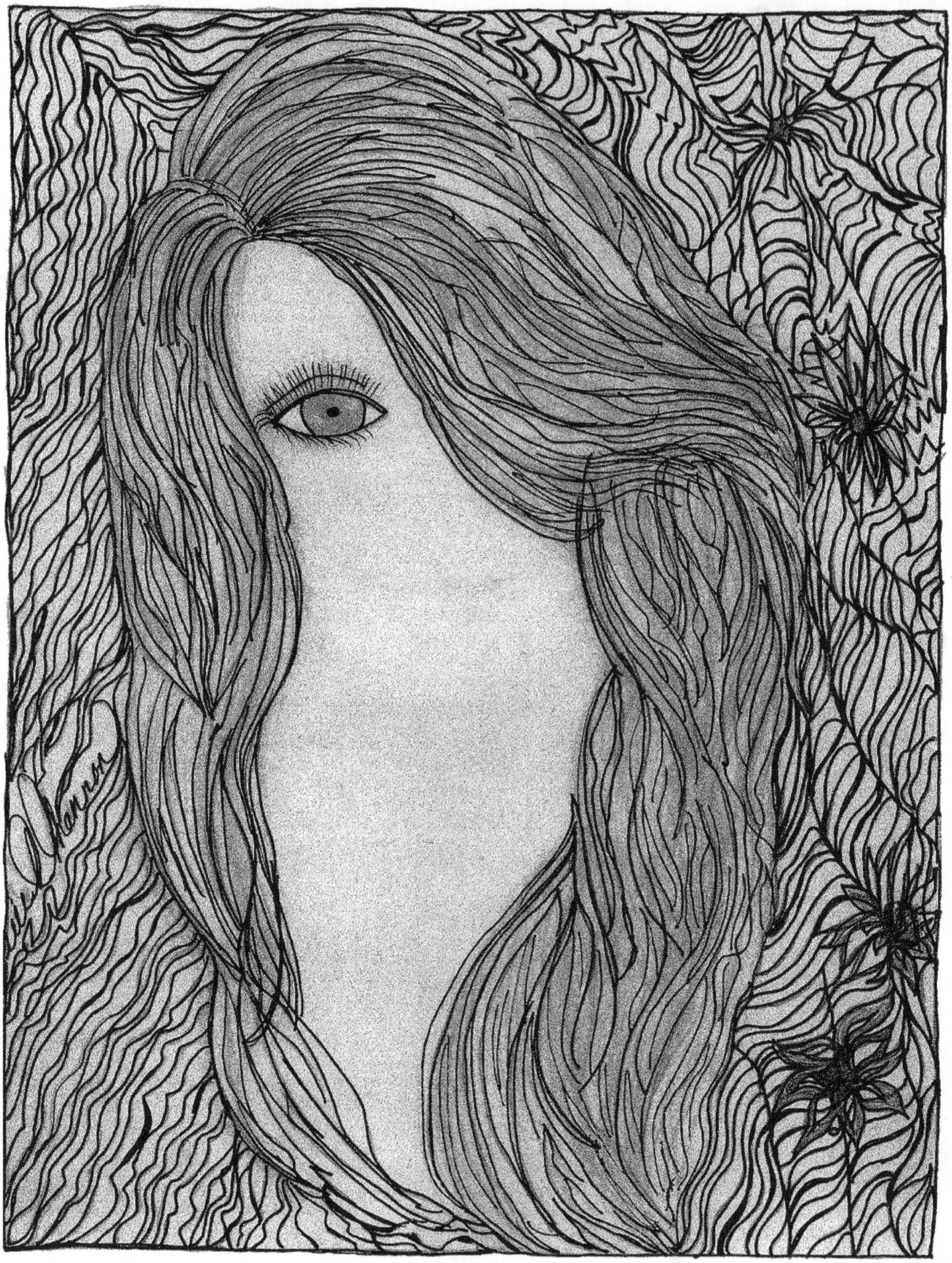

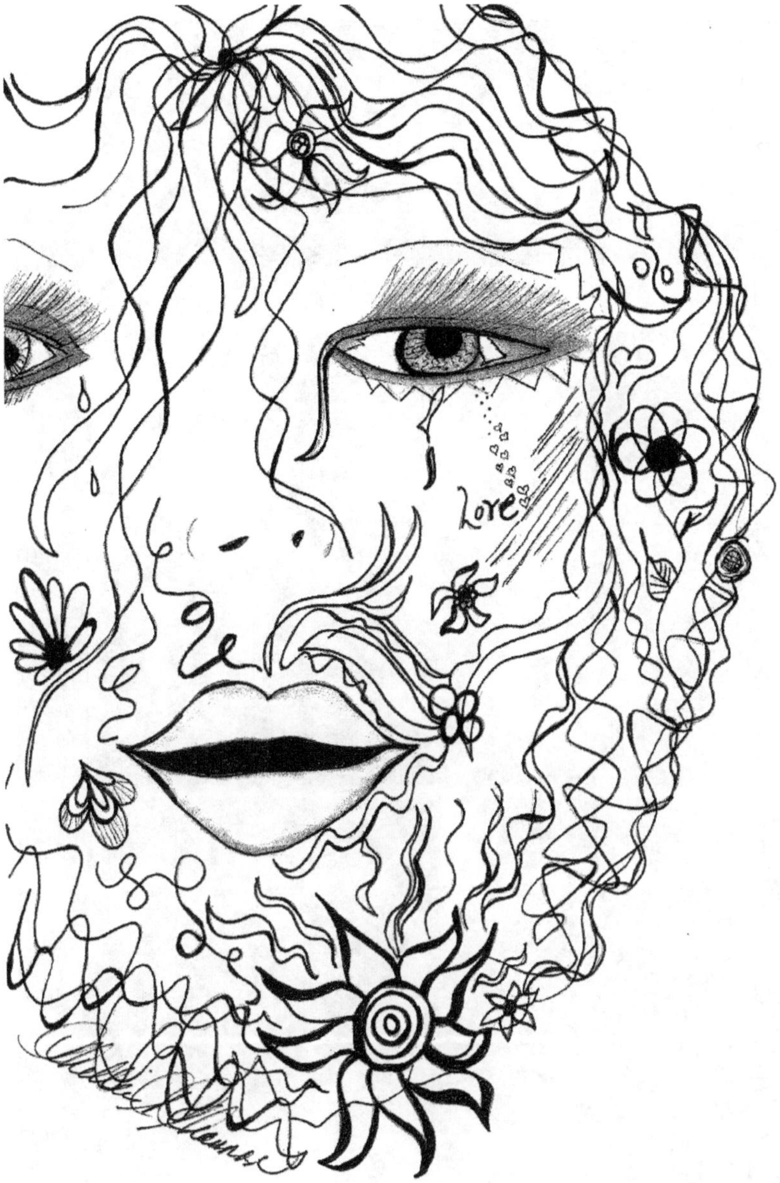
Love

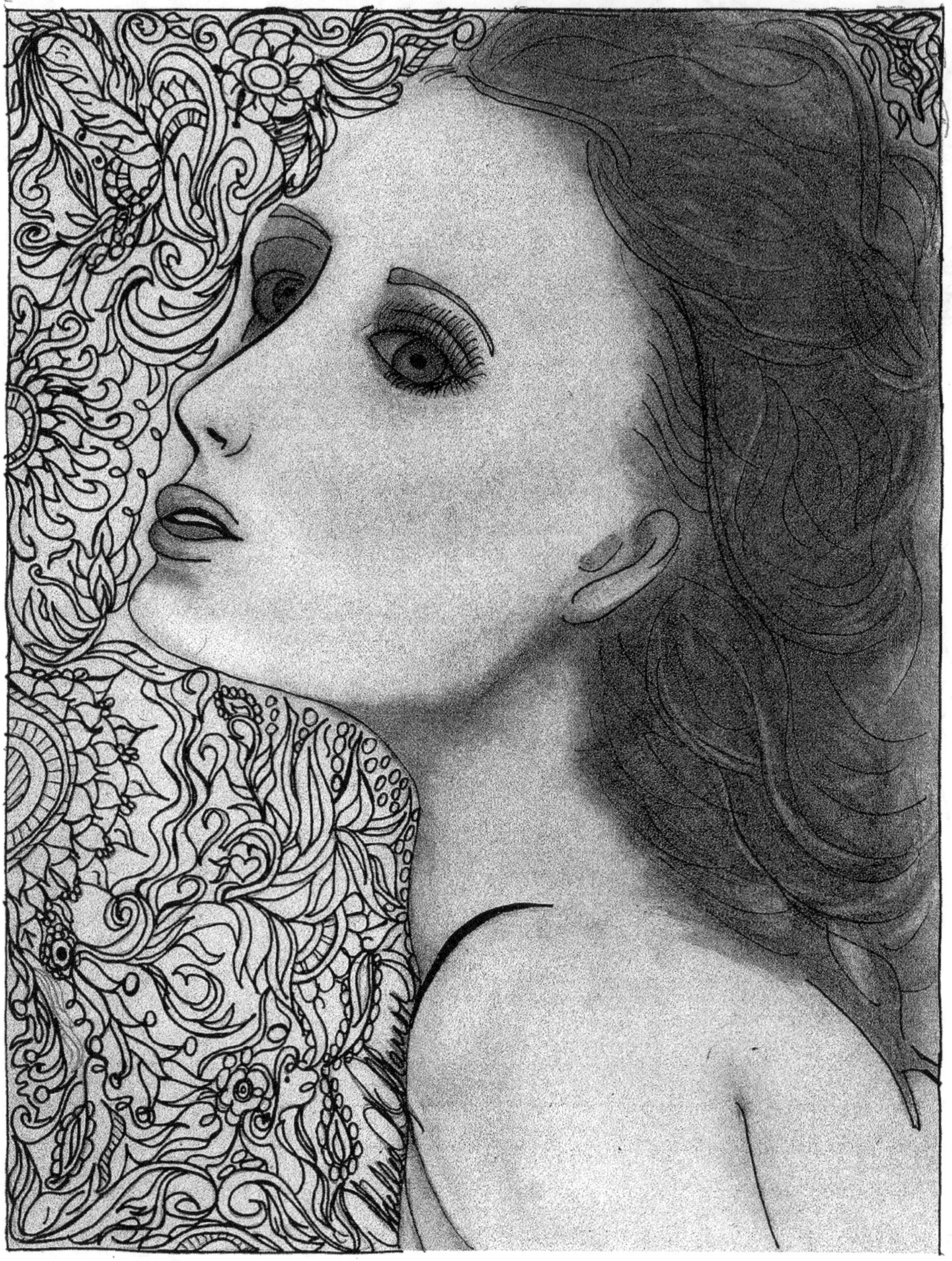

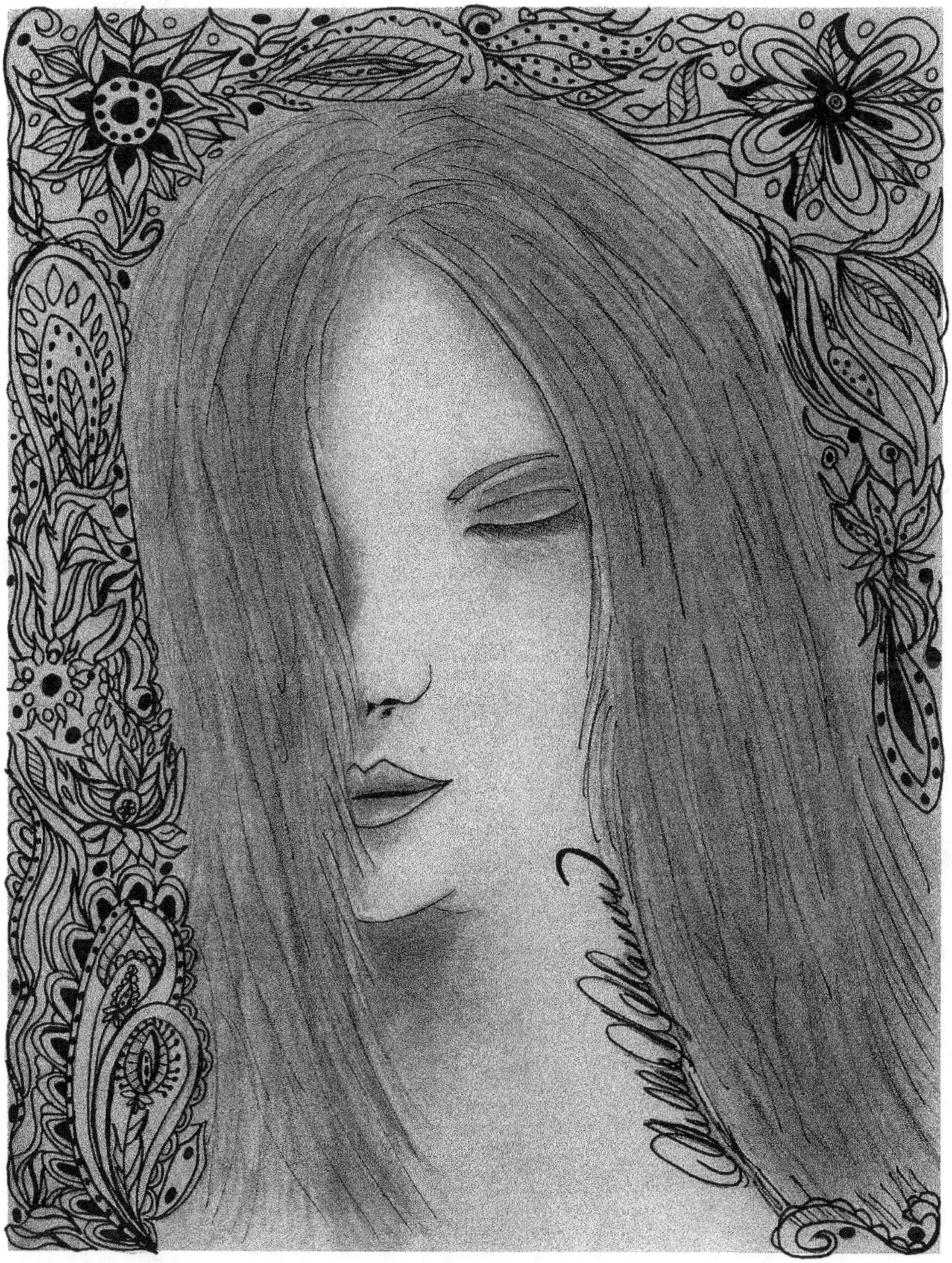

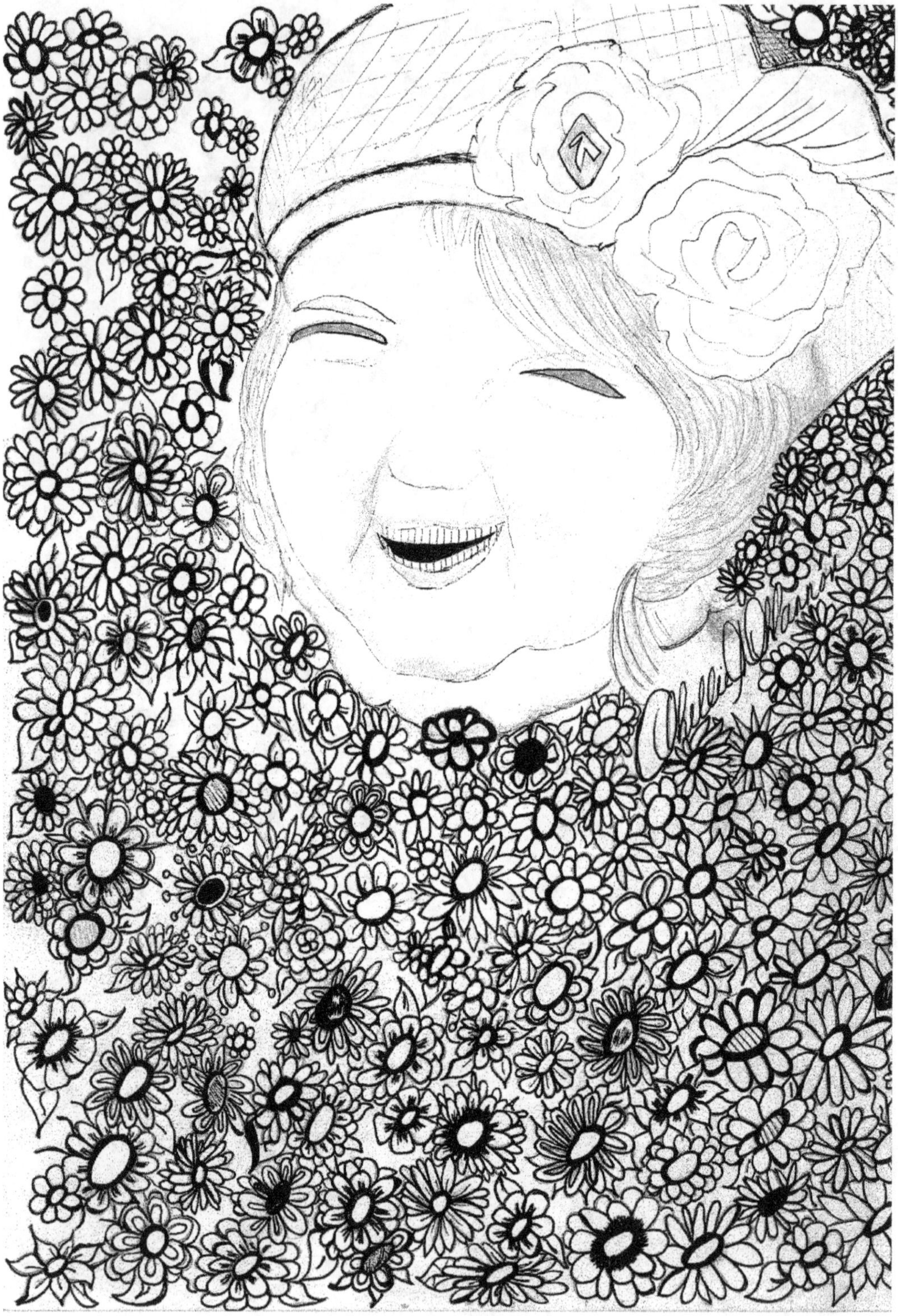

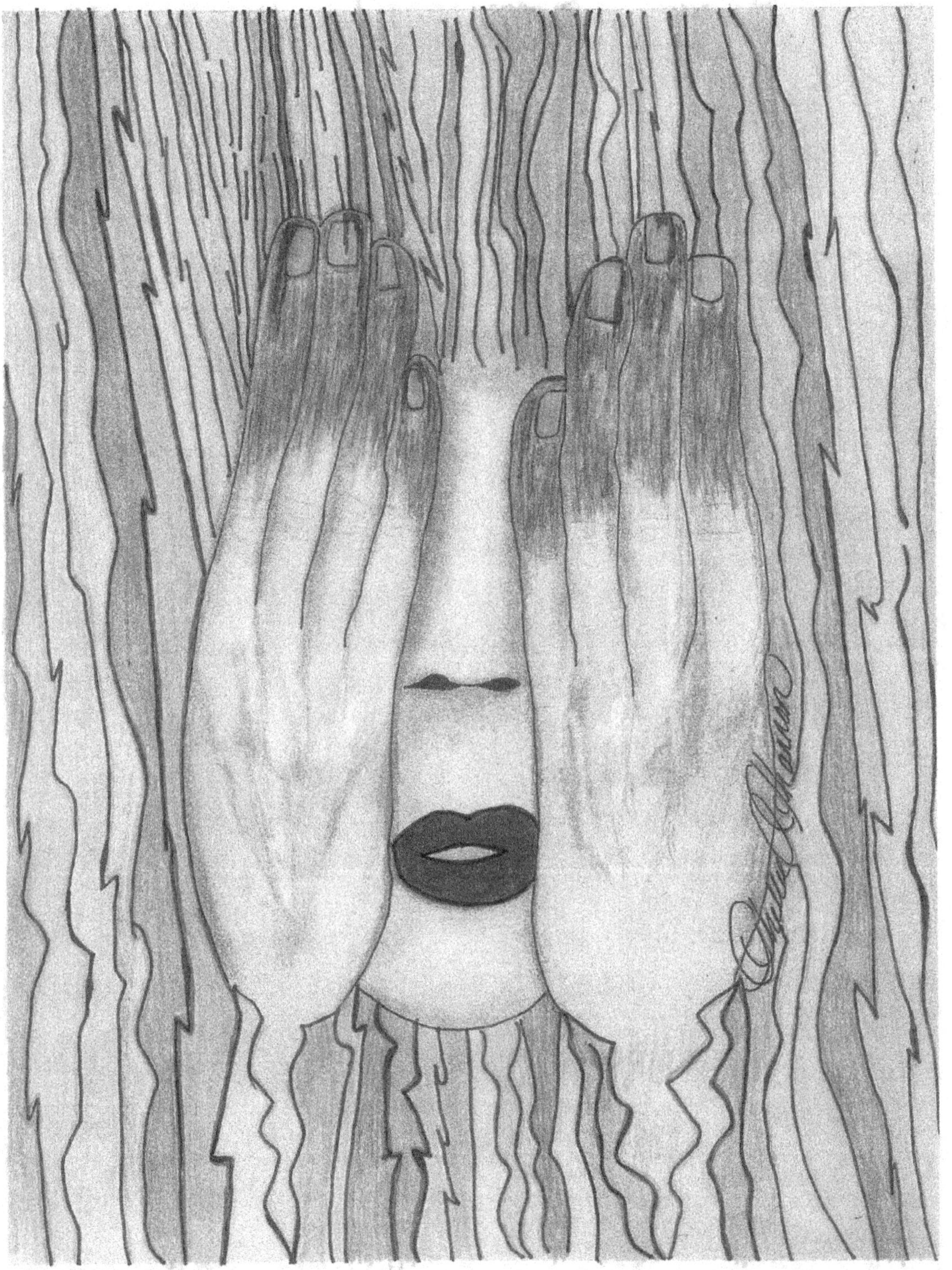

www.ingramcontent.com/pod-product-compliance
Lightning Source LLC
Chambersburg PA
CBHW080600190526
45169CB00007B/2828
* 9 7 8 1 5 3 2 9 3 8 1 9 1 *